the creative woman

By Debbie Mumm®

Celebrate your creativity with more than thirty projects that honor the creative woman in all of us! On every page, you'll find lots of inspiration for your next creative project!

contents

The Creative Woman...

Quilts

Scrapbooks

Cooks

Relaxes

Stitches

Enjoys Nature

Decorates

Gardens

The Creative Woman
Quilts

QUILTS
- celebrate our love for home and family,
- are a symbol of warmth and comfort,
- reflect our lives and dreams,
- honor our heritage,
- foster friendships and camaraderie,
- bring peace and fulfillment,
- express our innate creativity!

Made from scraps of satin party dresses and silks and velvets saved in a drawer over a lifetime of careful conservation, this crazy quilt was embroidered by a group of women gathered at a home following a funeral. The companionship brought comfort, the fabric inspired memories, and the needlework brought the joy of creative expression. ▶

It's amazing how much a few scraps of fabric and a little thread can do when in the hands of a creative woman!

Viola Schenk with her granddaughters Teri, Julie and Laura in 1968

My earliest memories are those of my Grandma, Viola. What I remember most are her hands. They were aged and scarred from a hard life, but her warm and gentle touch was full of love. When I hold and touch the things she made for me, I feel her love and remember her worn and tired hands. Those hands never stopped; whether it was sewing, quilting, crocheting, knitting, crafting, or needlepoint, she did it all! Now that she is gone, all I have to do is look at my hands, and I see her. She gave me her gift, the gift to create love with my hands.
~Julie Gutierrez

Scrap Basket Bed Quilt

Scrap Basket Bed Quilt 95" x 95"		FIRST CUT		SECOND CUT	
		Number of Strips or Pieces	Dimensions	Number of Pieces	Dimensions
Fabric A *Block One Background* 2⅜ yards		5 23	4½" x 42" 2½" x 42"	36 36 72 72	4½" squares 2½" x 8½" 2½" x 4½" 2½" squares
Fabric B *Block One Red Fabric* 1⅞ yards		6 14	4½" x 42" 2½" x 42"	45 216	4½" squares 2½" squares
Fabric C *Block Two Background* 1⅛ yards		2 10	4½" x 42" 2½" x 42"	16 16 32 32	4½" squares 2½" x 8½" 2½" x 4½" 2½" squares
Fabric D *Block One Corners & Block Two Red Fabric* 1⅛ yards		3 9	4½" x 42" 2½" x 42"	20 132	4½" squares 2½" squares
Fabric E *Block Three Background* 1⅞ yards		4 17	4½" x 42" 2½" x 42"	30 24 24 120	4½" squares 2½" x 8½" 2½" x 4½" 2½" squares
Fabric F *Block Three Red Fabric* 1⅛ yards		3 9	4½" x 42" 2½" x 42"	24 48 48	4½" squares 2½" x 4½" 2½" squares
Fabric G *Block Four Background* 1⅞ yards		4 17	4½" x 42" 2½" x 42"	30 24 24 120	4½" squares 2½" x 8½" 2½" x 4½" 2½" squares
Fabric H *Block Two Corners & Block Four Red Fabric* 1⅙ yards		3 10	4½" x 42" 2½" x 42"	24 48 64	4½" squares 2½" x 4½" 2½" squares
BORDERS					
First Border ½ yard		9	1½" x 42"		
Second Border ½ yard		9	1½" x 42"		
Third Border ½ yard		9	1½" x 42"		
Outside Border 1⅓ yards		10	4½" x 42"		
Binding ⅞ yard		10	2¾" x 42"		

Backing - 8⅔ yards
Batting - 103" x 103"

Cutting Instructions

Read all instructions before beginning and use ¼"-wide seam allowances throughout. Read Cutting Strips and Pieces on page 108 prior to cutting fabrics.

Getting Started

This quilt consists of two different blocks each measuring 16½" square unfinished. Blocks One and Two are exactly the same, just pieced in different fabrics with lights and darks rearranged. You will need nine of Block One and four of Block Two. Blocks Three and Four are also "twins," distinguished only by their different fabrics; you will make six of each. We've identified the top and side edges of each block so pressed seams oppose each other when the blocks are joined to make the quilt top.

Refer to Accurate Seam Allowance on page 108. Whenever possible, use the Assembly Line Method on page 108. Press seams in direction of arrows.

Block One

1. Refer to Quick Corner Triangles on page 108. Sew one 4½" Fabric A square to one 4½" Fabric B square as shown. Press. Make thirty-six.

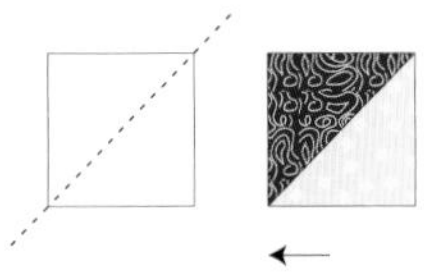

A = 4½ x 4½
B = 4½ x 4½
Make 36

2. Making quick corner triangle units, sew two 2½" Fabric B squares to one 2½" × 4½" Fabric A piece as shown. Press. Make seventy-two.

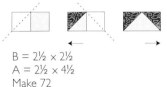

B = 2½ × 2½
A = 2½ × 4½
Make 72

3. Sew two units from step 2 together as shown. Press. Make thirty-six.

Make 36

4. Sew one unit from step 3 between two units from step 1 as shown. Press. Make eighteen.

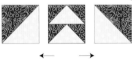

Make 18

5. Sew one 4½" Fabric B square between two units from step 3 as shown. Press. Make nine.

4½

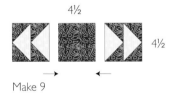

4½

Make 9

6. Sew one unit from step 5 between two units from step 4 as shown. Press. Make nine.

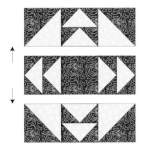

Make 9

7. Making a quick corner triangle unit, sew one 2½" Fabric A square to one 2½" Fabric B square as shown. Press. Make seventy-two.

A = 2½ × 2½
B = 2½ × 2½
Make 72

8. Sew one 2½" × 8½" Fabric A piece between two units from step 7 as shown. Press. Make thirty-six.

8½

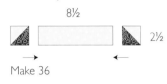

2½

Make 36

9. Sew one unit from step 6 between two units from step 8 as shown. Press. Make nine.

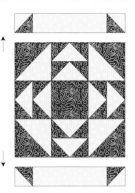

Make 9

Scrap Basket Bed Quilt
Finished size: 95" × 95"
Photo: page 4

10. Sew one unit from step 8 between two 2½" Fabric D squares as shown. Press. Make eighteen.

Make 18

11. Sew one unit from Step 9 between two units from Step 10 as shown. Press. Make nine blocks. Block One measures 16½" square.

Top of Block One

Side

Make 9
Block One measures 16½" square

Block Two

1. Refer to Quick Corner Triangles on page 108. Sew one 4½" Fabric C square to one 4½" Fabric D square as shown. Press. Make sixteen.

C = 4½ x 4½
D = 4½ x 4½
Make 16

2. Making quick corner triangle units, sew two 2½" Fabric D squares to one 2½" x 4½" Fabric C piece as shown. Press. Make thirty-two.

D = 2½ x 2½
C = 2½ x 4½
Make 32

3. Sew two units from step 2 together as shown. Press. Make sixteen.

Make 16

4. Sew one unit from step 3 between two units from step 1 as shown. Press. Make eight.

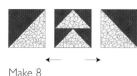

Make 8

5. Sew one 4½" Fabric D square between two units from step 3 as shown. Press. Make four.

4½

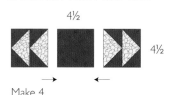

4½

Make 4

6. Sew one unit from step 5 between two units from step 4 as shown. Press. Make four.

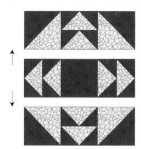

Make 4

7. Making a quick corner triangle unit, sew one 2½" Fabric C square to one 2½" Fabric D square as shown. Press. Make thirty-two.

C = 2½ x 2½
D = 2½ x 2½
Make 32

8. Sew 2½" x 8½" Fabric C piece between two units from step 7 as shown. Press. Make sixteen.

8½

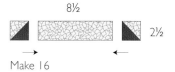

2½

Make 16

9. Sew one unit from step 6 between two units from step 8 as shown. Press. Make four.

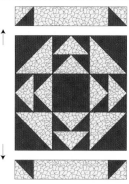

Make 4

10. Sew one unit from step 8 between two 2½" Fabric H squares as shown. Press. Make eight.

2½   2½

2½

Make 8

11. Sew unit from Step 9 between two units from Step 10 as shown. Press. Make four blocks. Block Two measures 16½" square.

Top of Block Two

Side

Make 4
Block Two measures 16½" square

The Creative Woman By Debbie Mumm®

Block Three and Block Four

1. Refer to Quick Corner Triangles on page 108. Sew one 4½" Fabric E square to one 4½" Fabric F square as shown. Press. Make twenty-four. Repeat using 4½" Fabric G and 4½" Fabric H squares. Make twenty-four.

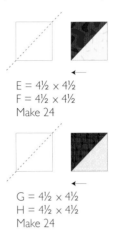

E = 4½ × 4½
F = 4½ × 4½
Make 24

G = 4½ × 4½
H = 4½ × 4½
Make 24

2. Making quick corner triangle units, sew two 2½" Fabric E squares to 2½" × 4½" Fabric F piece as shown. Press. Make forty-eight. Repeat using 2½" Fabric G squares and 2½" × 4½" Fabric H piece. Make forty-eight.

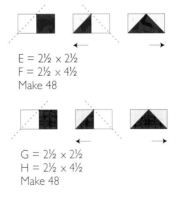

E = 2½ × 2½
F = 2½ × 4½
Make 48

G = 2½ × 2½
H = 2½ × 4½
Make 48

3. Sew two matching units from step 2 together as shown. Press. Make twenty-four of each color combination.

Make 24   Make 24

4. Sew one unit from step 3 between two matching units from step 1 as shown. Press. Make twelve of each color combination.

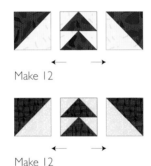

Make 12

Make 12

5. Sew one 4½" Fabric E square between two matching units from step 3 as shown. Press. Make six. Repeat using one 4½" Fabric G square and two matching units from step 3. Make six.

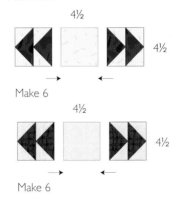

4½
4½
Make 6

4½
4½
Make 6

6. Sew one unit from step 5 between two matching units from step 4 as shown. Press. Make twelve, six of each combination.

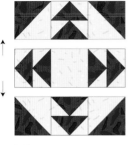

Make 6

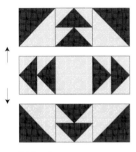

Make 6

7. Making a quick corner triangle unit, sew one 2½" Fabric E square to one 2½" Fabric F square as shown. Press. Make twenty-four. Repeat using 2½" Fabric G and 2½" Fabric H squares. Make twenty-four.

E = 2½ × 2½
F = 2½ × 2½
Make 24

G = 2½ × 2½
H = 2½ × 2½
Make 24

8. Sew 2½" × 8½" Fabric E piece between two matching units from step 7 as shown. Press. Make twelve. Repeat using one 2½" × 8½" Fabric G piece and two matching units from step 7. Make twelve.

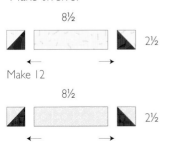

8½
2½
Make 12

8½
2½
Make 12

9. Sew one unit from step 6 between two matching units from step 8 as shown. Press. Make twelve, six of each combination.

Make 6

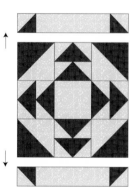

Make 6

10. Making a quick corner triangle unit, sew 2½" Fabric F square to 2½" × 4½" Fabric E piece as shown. Make twelve. Repeat using 2½" Fabric H squares and 2½" × 4½" Fabric G pieces. Make twelve.

F = 2½ × 2½
E = 2½ × 4½
Make 12

H = 2½ × 2½
G = 2½ × 4½
Make 12

11. Making a quick corner triangle unit, sew one 2½" Fabric F square to one 2½" × 4½" Fabric E piece as shown. Press. Make twelve. Repeat using one 2½" Fabric H square and one 2½" × 4½" Fabric G piece. Make twelve.

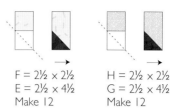

F = 2½ × 2½   H = 2½ × 2½
E = 2½ × 4½   G = 2½ × 4½
Make 12   Make 12

12. Sew one 2½" × 8½" Fabric E piece between matching units from steps 10 and 11 as shown. Press. Make twelve. Repeat using 2½" × 8½" Fabric G piece and matching units from steps 10 and 11. Make twelve.

Make 12   Make 12

13. Sew each unit from step 9 between two matching units from step 12 as shown. Press. Make six of each combination. Blocks Three and Four measure 16½" square.

Top of Block Three

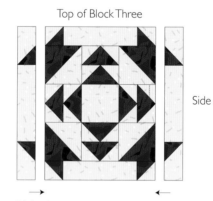

Side

Make 6
Block Three measures 16½" square

Top of Block Four

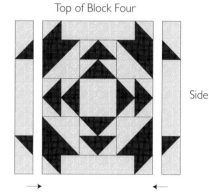

Side

Make 6
Block Four measures 16½" square

Assembly

1. Refer to photo on page 4 and layout on page 7. Arrange blocks in five horizontal rows of five blocks each as shown. Rows 1, 3, and 5 consist of three of Block One and two of Block Three. Rows 2 and 4 consist of two of Block Two and three of Block Four.

2. Sew blocks together to make rows. Press seams in opposite directions from row to row.

3. Sew rows together. Press.

The Creative Woman By Debbie Mumm®

Borders

1. Sew 1½" × 42" First Border strips end-to-end to make one continuous 1½"-wide strip. Press. Refer to Adding the Borders on page 110. Measure quilt through center from side to side. Cut two 1½"-wide First Border strips to that measurement. Sew to top and bottom of quilt. Press seams toward border.

2. Measure quilt through center from top to bottom, including borders just added. Cut two 1½"-wide First Border strips to that measurement. Sew to sides of quilt. Press.

3. Refer to steps 1 and 2 to join, measure, trim, and sew 1½"-wide Second Border strips, 1½"-wide Third Border strips, and 4½"-wide Outside Border strips to top, bottom, and sides of quilt. Press seams toward newly added borders.

Layering and Finishing

1. Cut backing crosswise into three equal pieces. Sew pieces together to make one 104" × 120" (approximate) backing piece. Cut backing to 104" × 104".

2. Arrange and baste backing, batting, and top together, referring to Layering the Quilt on page 110.

3. Hand or machine quilt as desired.

4. Sew 2¾" × 42" binding strips end-to-end to make one continuous 2¾"-wide strip. Refer to Binding the Quilt on page 110 and bind quilt to finish.

A quilter's bed deserves a special quilt, and this cozy charmer fills the bill perfectly. Two different blocks, each done in two different fabric combinations, create a kaleidoscope of secondary patterns. Although it may look complex, this design goes together almost effortlessly with our quick-cutting and piecing techniques.

Baskets & Blooms Wall Quilt

Finished size: 35" x 41"

How could a quilter—or anyone!—not be charmed by the cheerful blossoms in this sweet and scrappy wall quilt?

Cutting Instructions

Read all instructions before beginning and use ¼"-wide seam allowances throughout. Read Cutting Strips and Pieces on page 108 prior to cutting fabrics.

Getting Started

This quilt features four Basket Blocks, each made with two different fabrics and set on point. Blocks measure 9" square unfinished. Oversized triangles frame the medallion-style center and are trimmed after the center unit is assembled. Two double rows of Flying Geese and three borders in varying widths finish the quilt top. The quilt is bound on all four sides and the bottom edge is embellished with fifteen scrappy prairie points. Appliquéd flowers are fused and finished with decorative machine stitching.

Refer to Accurate Seam Allowance on page 108. Whenever possible, use the Assembly Line Method on page 108. Press seams in direction of arrows.

Basket Blocks

1. Refer to Quick Corner Triangles on page 108. Sew one 7¼" Fabric B square to one 7¼" Fabric C square as shown. Press. Make four, one of each combination. Reserve Fabric C scraps for handles.

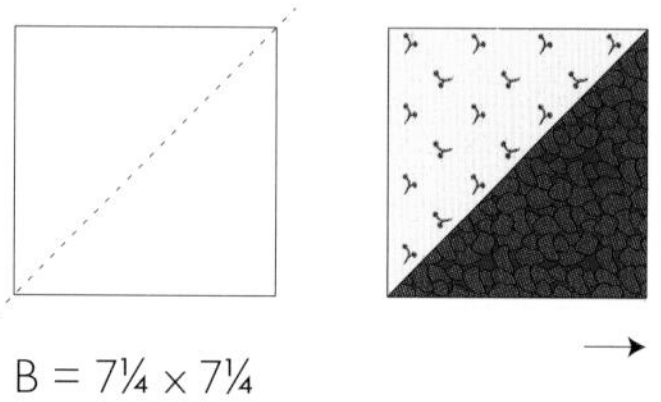

B = 7¼ x 7¼
C = 7¼ x 7¼
Make 4
(1 of each combination)

Baskets & Blooms Wall Quilt 35" x 41"		FIRST CUT	
		Number of Strips or Pieces	Dimensions
Fabric A *Background Setting Triangles* ½ yard		2	13" squares
Fabric B *Basket & Flying Geese Backgrounds* ⅓ yard **each** of four fabrics		1* 2* 3* 16*	7¼" square 2¼" x 5½" 2¼" squares 2" squares
		Cut for each fabric	
Fabric C *Baskets & Flying Geese* ⅓ yard **each** of four fabrics		1* 2* 8*	7¼" square 2¼" squares 2" x 3½"
		Cut for each fabric	

Baskets & Blooms Wall Quilt continued		FIRST CUT	
		Number of Strips or Pieces	Dimensions
BORDERS			
First Border ⅙ yard		4	1" x 42"
Second Border ¼ yard		4	1½" x 42"
Outside Border ½ yard		4	4" x 42"
Binding ⅜ yard		4	2¾" x 42"

Backing - 1½ yards
Batting - 39" x 45"
Handle Appliqués - Fabric C scraps
Flower Appliqués - Assorted tan, green & yellow scraps
Prairie Points - Assorted tan, red & green scraps for fifteen 4" squares
Lightweight Fusible Web - ⅓ yard

2. Making a quick corner triangle unit, sew one 2¼" Fabric B square to one 2¼" Fabric C square as shown. Press. Make eight, two of each combination.

B = 2¼ × 2¼
C = 2¼ × 2¼
Make 8
(2 of each combination)

3. Sew 2¼" × 5½" Fabric B piece to matching unit from step 2. Press. Make four, one of each combination.

5½

2¼

Make 4
(1 of each combination)

4. Sew unit from step 3 to matching unit from step 1. Press. Make four, one of each combination.

Make 4
(1 of each combination)

5. Sew unit from step 2 between matching 2¼" Fabric B square and 2¼" × 5½" Fabric B piece. Press. Make four, one of each combination.

2¼   5½

2¼

Make 4
(1 of each combination)

6. Sew unit from step 5 to matching unit from step 4. Press. Make four, one of each combination. Block measures 9" square.

Make 4
(1 of each combination)
Block measures 9" square

Flying Geese Units

1. Refer to Quick Corner Triangles on page 108. Sew matching 2" Fabric B squares to 2" × 3½" Fabric C piece as shown. Press. Make thirty-two, eight of each combination.

B = 2 × 2
C = 2 × 3½
Make 32
(8 of each combination)

2. Sew two matching units from step 1 together as shown. Press. Make sixteen, four of each combination.

Make 16
(4 of each combination)

Baskets & Blooms Wall Quilt
Finished size: 35" × 41"
Photo: page 12

3. Sew eight units from step 2 to make a horizontal row as shown. Press. Make two.

Make 2

Assembly

1. Refer to photo on page 12 and layout on page 13. Arrange and sew Basket Blocks together in pairs. Press seams in opposite directions in each pair. Sew pairs together to make a square. Press.

Make 2 (one of each combination)

2. Cut each 13" Fabric A square in half once diagonally to make two triangles. Sew triangles to opposites sides of unit from step 1. (Note: Triangles will extend past raw edges of square.) Press seams toward triangles. Sew triangles to remaining sides. Press. Square unit, if necessary, to measure 24½" square.

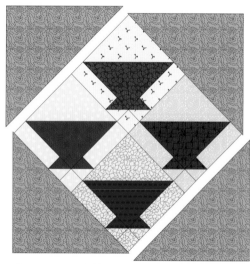

Square unit to 24½".

3. Refer to photo on page 12 and layout on page 13. Sew unit from step 2 between Flying Geese rows. Press seams toward center.

Borders

1. Refer to Adding the Borders on page 110. Measure quilt through center from side to side. Cut two 1" × 42" First Border strips to that measurement. Sew to top and bottom of quilt. Press seams toward borders.

2. Measure quilt through center from top to bottom, including borders just added. Cut two 1"-wide First Border strips to that measurement. Sew to sides of quilt. Press.

3. Refer to steps 1 and 2 to measure, trim, and sew 1½"-wide Second Border and 4"-wide Outside Border strips to top, bottom, and sides of quilt. Press seams toward borders.

Adding the Appliqués

Refer to appliqué instructions on page 109. Our instructions are for Quick-Fuse Appliqué. If you prefer hand appliqué, add ¼"-wide seam allowance to templates.

1. Trace appliqué patterns on page 15 for basket handle, flower, and flower center. Cut one handle from each Fabric C scrap and sixteen flowers and flower centers from assorted tan, green, and yellow fabric scraps.

2. Refer to photo on page 12 and layout on page 13. Position and fuse appliqués in place and finish with satin stitch or decorative stitching as desired.

Layering and Finishing

1. Arrange and baste backing, batting, and top together, referring to Layering the Quilt on page 110.

2. Hand or machine quilt as desired.

3. To make prairie points, fold and press one 4" tan, red, or green square in half diagonally, wrong sides together as shown. Fold and press diagonally in half again as shown to make a prairie point. Make fifteen in assorted colors.

Make 15
in assorted tans, reds and greens

4. Refer to photo on page 12 and layout on page 13. With right sides together and raw edges aligned, arrange prairie points along bottom edge of quilt. Baste.

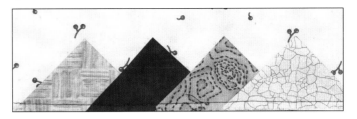

5. Sew 2¾" x 42" binding strips end-to-end to make one continuous 2¾"-wide strip. Trim batting and backing to ¼" beyond raw edge of quilt top only at top and side edges. On bottom edge of quilt, trim batting and backing even with raw edge of prairie points.

6. Refer to Binding the Quilt on page 110, steps 2-5, to bind quilt. In step 5 of Binding the Quilt, press bottom seam and binding to back of quilt and prairie points away from quilt. The bottom binding will be wider on the back of quilt, but will allow prairie points to lay flat.

Baskets & Blooms Appliqué Patterns

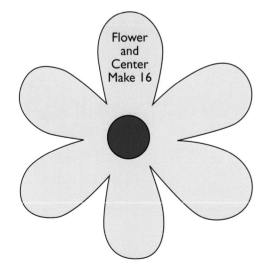

Flower
and
Center
Make 16

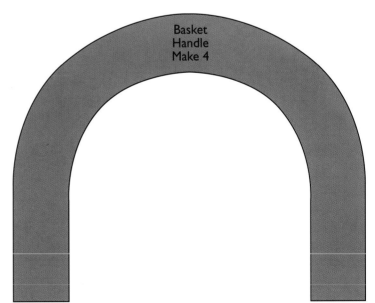

Basket
Handle
Make 4

Hand Quilter's Pillow

Finished size: 19" square

Show off your very best quilting stitches on this elegant pillow. The beautiful curved quilting motif is a perfect counterpoint to the crisp geometry of the four-patch background and high contrast color palette.

Making the Pillow Top

1. Sew one 7" Fabric A square and one 7" Fabric B square together as shown. Press. Make two.

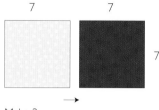

Make 2

2. Sew two units from step 1 together as shown. Press.

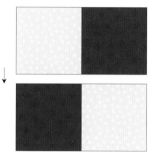

3. Refer to photo and layout. Sew unit from step 2 between two 1" × 13½" Fabric C strips. Press seams toward Fabric C. Sew 1" × 14½" Fabric C strips to remaining sides. Press.

4. Sew unit from step 3 between two 3" × 14½" Fabric B strips. Press seams toward Fabric B. Sew 3" × 19½" Fabric B strips to remaining sides. Press.

Cutting Instructions

Read all instructions before beginning and use ¼"-wide seam allowances throughout. Read Cutting Strips and Pieces on page 108 prior to cutting fabrics.

Getting Started

This pillow features a large four-patch block framed with two simple borders. The quilting motif is worked in red thread on the light squares and tan thread on the dark squares. Press seams in direction of arrows.

Hand Quilted Pillow 19" × 19"	FIRST CUT	
	Number of Strips or Pieces	Dimensions
Fabric A *Light Squares* ¼ yard	2	7" squares
Fabric B *Dark Squares, Outside Border, and Backing* ⅞ yard	2 2 2 2	12½" × 19½" (backing) 7" squares 3" × 19½" 3" × 14½"
Fabric C *First Border* ⅛ yard	2 2	1" × 14½" 1" × 13½"
Lining and Batting - 22½" square of each 19" Pillow Form		

Layering and Finishing

1. Copy quilting pattern below four times, aligning placement lines, to form a square quilting template. Referring to photo and layout, use your favorite method to transfer quilting template onto pillow top.

2. Refer to Finishing Pillows on page 111, step 1, to layer and quilt pillow top. We hand quilted the design, then added simple machine quilting to secure borders.

3. Refer to Finishing Pillows on page 111, steps 2–4, to sew backing to pillow.

4. Refer to Pillow Forms on page 111 to make 19" square pillow form, if desired.

Hand Quilter's Pillow
Finished size: 19" square
Photo: page 16

Quilting Pattern

Tracing Line————————
Placement Line – – – – – – –

Center

The Creative Woman

Scrapbooks

Scraps....Scrapbooking....
There's a reason that scrapbooking begins with scraps! Like quilting, scrapbooking takes the bits and pieces of our lives and arranges them in beautiful and elegant patterns to be enjoyed by generations to come.
Both quilting and scrapbooking celebrate the joys of family and friendships and preserve precious memories.

Important days or special occasions can be commemorated in cloth with a memory quilt or treasured with a special display in a scrapbook. When a group gets together for a crop night or a quilting bee, the ideas fly, the conversation rumbles, friendships form, and projects reflect the joy and excitement of companionship.

Kathy Rickel with Baby Brian's quilt

Friends gather for a crop night, sharing ideas and friendship and proudly displaying finished pages!

Scrapbookers Mya Brooks, Georgie Gerl, Heather Butler, Sabrina Gonder, Kris Clifford, and Kathy Eisenbarth

At the Debbie Mumm Studio, special occasions are commemorated with a group quilt and a scrapbook page recording the surprise presentation! A new baby was celebrated with this special quilt. Each staff member made a block, then everyone gathered together to sew and finish the milestone-marking heirloom!

Just as pieces stitched together in a quilt warm our spirit, scrapbooks bind memories together to warm our hearts.

Memories Lap Quilt

Memories Lap Quilt 65" x 65"	FIRST CUT		SECOND CUT	
	Number of Strips or Pieces	Dimensions	Number of Pieces	Dimensions
Fabric A *Center and Corner Signature Squares* ½ yard	2 1	4½" x 42" 3½" x 42"	16 9	4½" squares 3½" squares
Fabric B *Stacked Squares* ⅝ yard each of nine fabrics	2* 1* 1*	5" x 42" 4" x 42" 3" x 42"	2* 2* 2* 2* 2* 2*	5" x 17½" 5" x 8½" 4" x 12½" 4" x 5½" 3" x 8½" 3" x 3½"
		Cut for each fabric		
Fabric C *Sashing* ¾ yard	16	1½" x 42"		
Fabric D *Sashing* ⅝ yard	8	2½" x 42"		
BORDERS				
First Border ½ yard	6	2" x 42"		
Outside Border 1 yard	6	5" x 42"		
Binding ⅝ yard	7	2¾" x 42"		
Backing - 4 yards Batting - 71" x 71"				

Cutting Instructions

Read all instructions before beginning and use ¼"-wide seam allowances throughout. Read Cutting Strips and Pieces on page 108 prior to cutting fabrics.

Getting Started

This quilt consists of nine Signature Blocks, measuring 12½" square unfinished. Each features a 3½" center square that can be signed either before or after the blocks are constructed. If you wish, the 4½" corner squares can be signed as well. Mix and match Fabric B from block to block for a playful, scrappy look.

Refer to Accurate Seam Allowance on page 108. Whenever possible, use the Assembly Line Method on page 108. Press seams in direction of arrows.

Signature Blocks

1. Sew one 3½" Fabric A square between two 3" x 3½" Fabric B pieces as shown. Press. Sew unit between two matching 3" x 8½" Fabric B pieces. Press. Make nine in assorted colors.

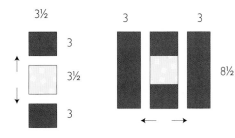

Make 9
(in assorted colors)

2. Randomly angle a square ruler over each unit, and trim two sides as shown. Square unit to 5½" by rotating ruler to trim remaining two sides as shown. Vary angle of ruler for each unit to give a scrapbook effect. Make nine.

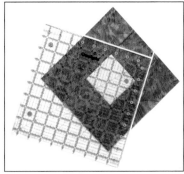

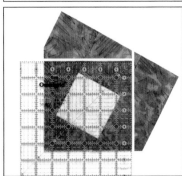

Make 9
Trim to 5½" square

3. Sew unit from step 2 between two 4" × 5½" Fabric B strips. Press seams toward strips. Sew two matching 4" × 12½" Fabric B strips to remaining sides. Press. Make nine in assorted colors.

4. Repeat step 2 to trim each unit from step 3 to 8½" square as shown. Make nine.

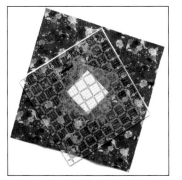

Make 9
Trim to 8½" square

5. Sew unit from step 4 between two 5" × 8½" Fabric B strips. Press seams toward strips. Sew two matching 5" × 17½" Fabric B strips to remaining sides. Press. Make nine in assorted colors.

6. Repeat step 2 to trim each unit from step 5 to 12½" square to complete block as shown. Make nine.

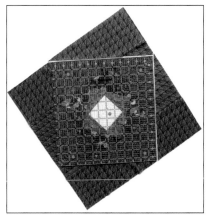

Make 9
Trim to 12½" square

Assembly

1. Sew one 2½" × 42" Fabric D strip between two 1½" × 42" Fabric C strips as shown. Press. Make eight.

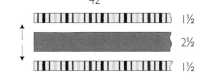

Make 8

2. Cut twenty-four 12½"-wide segments from strip sets as shown.

Cut 24 segments

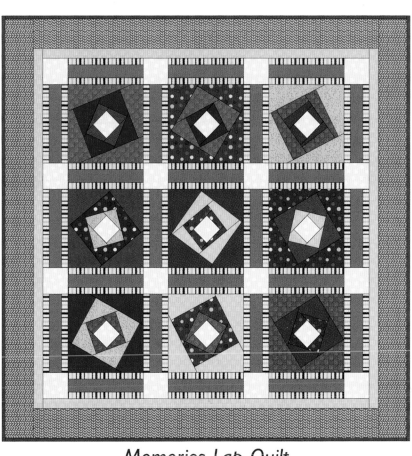

Memories Lap Quilt
Finished size: 65" × 65"
Photo: page 18

3. Sew four 4½" Fabric A squares and three segments from step 2 together as shown. Press. Make four.

4½   4½   4½   4½

4½

Make 4

4. Sew four segments from step 2 and three Signature Blocks together as shown to make a row. Press. Make three rows.

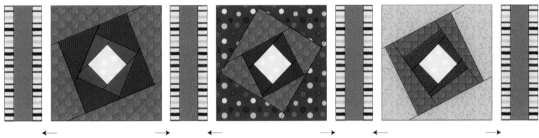

Make 3

5. Refer to layout on page 21 and photo. Arrange rows from steps 3 and 4, alternating as shown. Sew rows together. Press.

What better way to commemorate a special gathering, landmark date, or cherished group of family or friends than with this wonderful, whimsically-pieced signature quilt? The block centers and corner squares are perfect for signatures by wedding, anniversary, or reunion guests; by friends at a quilting retreat or weekly bee; or by students for a beloved teacher or coach.

Borders

1. Sew 2" × 42" First Border strips end-to-end to make one continuous 2"-wide strip. Press. Refer to Adding the Borders on page 110. Measure quilt through center from side to side. Cut two 2"-wide First Border strips to that measurement. Sew to top and bottom of quilt. Press seams toward borders.

2. Measure quilt through center from top to bottom, including borders just added. Cut two 2"-wide First Border strips to that measurement. Sew to sides of quilt. Press.

3. Refer to steps 1 and 2 to join, measure, trim, and sew 5"-wide Outside Border strips to top, bottom, and sides of quilt. Press.

Layering and Finishing

1. Cut backing crosswise into two equal pieces. Sew pieces together to make one 72" × 84" (approximate) backing piece. Press and trim to 72" × 72".

2. Arrange and baste backing, batting, and top together, referring to Layering the Quilt on page 110.

3. Hand or machine quilt as desired.

4. Sew 2¾" × 42" binding strips end-to-end to make one continuous 2¾"-wide strip. Refer to Binding the Quilt on page 110 and bind quilt to finish.

creative concepts

Heart to Hand Scrapbook Page

Finished size: 12" square

There is a creative woman in all of us and she needs to celebrate her passion! Why not showcase your unique contributions and accomplishments by documenting them in your scrapbook? Generations to come will appreciate your talent as a crafter, quilter, decorator, or scrapbooker.

Materials Needed

All products should be archive quality.

Assorted Scrapbook Papers - Red, grey, ivory, and motif
Alphabet Stickers
Assorted Stickers
Vellum Paper
Heart-Shaped Eyelets
Foam Mounting Tape
Black Pen
Craft Knife and Cutting Mat
Scrapbooking Glue
5" x 7" Photo

Making the Page

1. Using a craft knife and a cutting mat, cut out center of photo, leaving a ½" wide frame. Trim center photo an additional ⅛" around all four sides. Glue photo frame on grey paper. Mount photo in center of frame using foam mounting tape. Glue photo unit on red paper.

2. Tear a piece of grey paper to approximately 4" x 9".

3. Create page title using alphabet stickers on a 1½" x 7½" piece of vellum paper.

4. Attach vellum title strip to torn piece of grey paper using heart-shaped eyelets.

5. Write a quote or message on ivory paper using a black pen. Glue to title block.

6. Glue title block to bottom third of motif paper.

7. Glue mounted photo to top of page, overlapping title block slightly.

8. Complete page with a few stickers.

Recollections Wall Art

Finished size: 16" x 24" and two 11" squares

Display treasured times on your walls with this technique which combines sewing and scrapbooking to create unique art pieces.

Getting Started

A variety of scrapbooking, sewing, and painting techniques are used for this project. Refer to Garden Delight, Preparing the Stretched Canvas, pages 104-105, steps 1-3, to make canvas forms. Refer to step 4 to paint 16" x 24" and one 11" square canvas with Gesso. The other 11" canvas is covered with a pieced fabric unit instead of paint. Read all instructions before beginning.

Painting the Canvas

Using a 2"-wide bristle brush and medium green paint, paint 16" x 24" and one 11" square stretched canvas. Work quickly to cover top and sides. While paint is wet, lightly pull a whisk broom or scrub brush through paint in a vertical direction to create distinctive brush marks, adding texture to entire canvas. Allow to dry.

Friends in Nature

Finished Size: 16" x 24"

Additional Materials Needed

⅛ yard each of two fabrics
    One 3¼" x 28" piece
    Two 1½" x 28" pieces

4mm Silk Ribbon - gold, green, and gold variegated

Ten Assorted Beads

White Graphite Transfer Paper

General Materials Needed

Pre-made Stretcher Bars -
    Two 24" bars
    Two 16" bars
    Eight 11" bars

Lightweight Canvas -
    One 22" x 30" piece
    Two 17" squares

Staple Gun and Staples

Gesso

Acrylic Paint - Medium green

Paintbrush - 2"-wide bristle

Whisk Broom or Scrub Brush

Photos (Duplicate photos are recommended)

Cardstock - Gold and Black

Cork -
    One 4½" x 6¼" piece
    Two 3½" x 4¾" pieces

Foam Mounting Tape

Spray Adhesive

Rubber Cement

Assorted Needles

Assorted Buttons - Twelve

Vellum Paper

Additional materials are listed with individual projects.

TIP

Important Tip:

For tracing or gluing on stretched canvas forms, place ½" thick piece of wood or a book under canvas to provide a solid surface.

Instructions

1. Trace Ribbon Embroidery Pattern on page 26 onto paper.

2. Referring to photo, place embroidery pattern on canvas, making sure pattern is at least ½" inside stretcher bars. Place white graphite transfer paper under pattern and trace.

3. Referring to Embroidery Stitch Guide on page 111, use green silk ribbon and Lazy Daisy Stitch, to sew leaves on painted canvas.

4. For stem, pull silk ribbon through canvas to make one very long stitch. Use glue to hold stem in a slight curve. Use gold silk ribbon and Lazy Daisy Stitch to embroider dragonfly.

5. Refer to embroidery pattern on page 26 and photo to sew beads to canvas.

6. Sew one 3¼" × 28" fabric strip between two 1½" × 28" fabric strips. Press seams toward center.

7. Fold and press 28"-long side edges under ½".

8. Referring to photo, attach unit from step 7 to canvas by wrapping ends over top and bottom edges and stapling to frame.

9. Using rubber cement, glue 4½" × 6¼" cork piece to 4⅝ " × 6⅜" piece of black cardstock.

10. Print a favorite quote on vellum paper. Trim to 4" × 5¾". Center vellum on top of unit from step 9. Referring to photo on page 24, place vellum/cork unit on fabric strip and canvas. Sew a button in each corner through canvas and all layers to affix unit in place.

11. Cut gold card stock into three 3¾" × 6½" pieces. Referring to photo, attach 3¼" × 6" photos to card stock using foam mounting tape. Glue to canvas.

12. Referring to photo, use foam mounting tape to attach 6" × 8" photo to canvas.

Patches of Love
Finished Size: 11" square

Additional Materials Needed

Fabric Background Square - ½ yard
    One 15" square

Fabric Photo Mat - ⅙ yard
    One 11" x 7½"

Foam Core - ⅛-thick
    One 8" x 4½" piece

Instructions

1. Fold corners of 15" fabric square to center of wrong side of fabric to form a 10½" square. Press. Referring to photo, center fabric square on-point on 11" square painted canvas form and wrap ends over sides of canvas. Staple to back.

2. Using spray adhesive, cover one side of 8" × 4½" foam core with 11" × 7½" fabric piece, wrap edges and adhere fabric to back. Attach 7" × 3½" photo to unit using foam mounting tape. Using rubber cement, glue to canvas.

3. Using rubber cement, glue 3½" × 4½" cork piece to 3⅝" × 4⅝" piece of black cardstock. Print a favorite quote on vellum paper. Trim to 3" × 4". Center vellum on top of cork unit and referring to photo, place on canvas form. Sew a button in each corner through canvas and all layers to affix unit in place.

Work of Heart

Finished Size: 11" square

Additional Materials Needed

Fabrics - ⅛ yard each of ten assorted
- One 3¼" x 15" strip
- One 1¼" x 15" strip
- One 2¾" x 15" strip
- One 1⅜" x 15" strip
- One 2¼" x 15" strip
- One 1⅜" x 15" strip
- One 2¼" x 15" strip
- One 1⅜" x 15" strip
- One 1" x 15" strip
- One 3¼" x 15" strip

Trim - ½ yard of ⅜ "-wide

Ribbon - ½ yard each of ⅝ " and ½ "-wide

Instructions

1. Referring to photo, sew assorted fabric strips together in order listed in materials list. Press seams in one direction.

2. Referring to photo, sew trims to unit from step 1 as desired. (The ⅜"-wide black trim was sewn to second strip, ⅝"-wide gold ribbon to third strip, and ⅜"-wide red ribbon to seventh strip.)

3. Place fabric unit on canvas frame. Wrap edges over sides of canvas and staple to frame.

4. Cut two black cardstock pieces to 4" x 6" and 3⅝" x 4⅞". Using spray adhesive, attach photo to 4" x 6" piece.

5. Using rubber cement, glue matted photo to fabric background.

6. Using rubber cement, glue 3½" x 4¾" cork piece to 3⅝" x 4⅞" piece of black cardstock.

7. Print a favorite quote on vellum paper. Trim to 3" x 4¼". Center vellum on top of unit from step 6. Referring to photo, place vellum/cork unit of fabric wrapped form. Sew a button in each corner through all layers to affix unit in place.

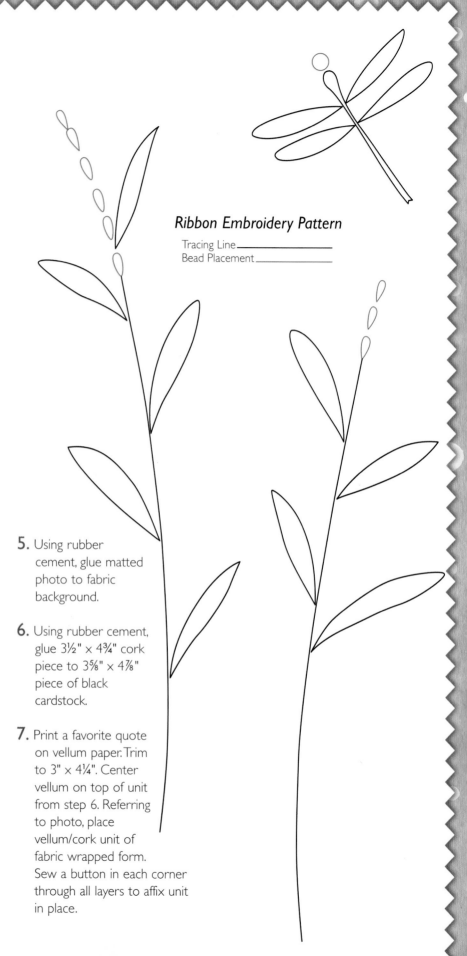

Ribbon Embroidery Pattern

Tracing Line_____
Bead Placement_____

Keepsake Pillow

Finished size: 20" square

Transfer a favorite photo to fabric to create a lasting keepsake that's both decorative and functional. The fabric photo transfer technique could also be used in plain blocks of the Memories Lap Quilt (page 20) if desired.

Materials Needed

Fabric A (Photo Center) -
(Closely woven white cotton fabric such as Pima cotton.)
  One 7" x 9" piece

Fabric B (Accent) - ⅛ yard
  Two ¾" x 7½" pieces
  Two ¾" x 5" pieces

Fabric C (Square) - ⅙ yard
  Two 4" x 14½" strips
  Two 4" x 5½" pieces

Fabric D (Square) - ⅜ yard
  Two 6" x 20" strips
  Two 6" x 9" pieces

First Border - ⅛ yard
  Two 1" x 14½" strips
  Two 1" x 13½" strips

Outside Border - ¼ yard
  Two 3½" x 20½" strips
  Two 3½" x 14½" strips

Backing - ⅝ yard
  Two 13" x 20½" pieces

Batting/Lining - ⅔ yard
  One 23" square each

14" Pillow Form

Photograph (5" x 7" image)

Making the Pillow

This project utilizes a fabric photo transfer technique. There are many different products and methods to transfer photos to fabric: photo transfer paper, direct printing onto fabric using a computer printer, cyanotype (exposure to ultraviolet light), and chemical transfers. Follow manufacturer's directions to transfer photo image to fabric,

paying close attention to correct procedure to "set" the ink. If not set properly, image may wash out with laundering. We selected a photo, reversed the image, and enlarged it on a color copier, printing directly onto the transfer paper. Read all instructions before beginning.

1. Transfer photo to 7" x 9" Fabric A piece using method of your choice. Trim fabric to 5" x 7".

2. Sew piece from step 1 between two ¾" x 5" Fabric B pieces. Press. Sew two ¾" x 7½" Fabric B pieces to remaining sides. Press.

3. Sew unit from step 2 between two 4" x 5½" Fabric C pieces. Press. Sew two 4" x 14½" Fabric C strips to remaining sides. Press.

4. Referring to photo and Memories Lap Quilt Signature Blocks, page 20, step 2, position and trim unit to 9" square.

5. Sew unit from step 4 between two 6" x 9" Fabric D pieces. Press. Sew two 6" x 20" Fabric D strips to remaining sides. Press. Position and trim unit to 13½" square, making sure photo is straight and centered.

6. Sew 1" x 13½" and 1" x 14½" First Border strips and 3½" x 14½" and 3½" x 20½" Outside Border strips to top, bottom, and sides of unit from step 5. Press seams toward border just sewn.

7. Refer to Finishing Pillows on page 111, step 1, to quilt pillow. Refer to steps 2-4 to sew 13" x 20½" Backing pieces to pillow. Stitch-in-the-ditch between First and Outside Border to create a flange. Insert 14" square pillow form.

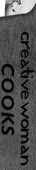

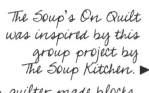

The Creative Woman Cooks

A soup pot is always simmering on the kitchen stove when The Soup Kitchen Quilters meet!

Recognizing how lucky they were to be able to enjoy good food and the companionship of friends led this group to reach out internationally to women in crisis with the comfort and hope of quilting. Matthew, the nephew of one of the quilters, was working in a refugee camp in eastern Hungary. Scarred by innumerable tragedies, women from Afghanistan, Iran, and Iraq had gathered at this camp for safety and to provide basic necessities for their children. The Soup Kitchen Quilters decided to not only send comforting quilts to the camp, but also to send supplies, information, and instructions to help the women make their own quilts and, possibly, learn a livelihood for an uncertain future.

The results of their efforts were eloquently described by Matthew.... "The day that we gave the quilts to these women was a much needed time of joy and security for the women. They were so grateful and proud. They adored the colors and talked about the patterns endlessly. They wrapped the quilts tightly around their bodies and plunged their faces in the fabric to breathe in their gifts and their creators. They quickly went to work studying how to make their own quilts; the one woman who could read English well translated the instructions for the others..."

The Soup Kitchen Quilters—

Making a heartfelt connection by sharing quilts with women of a common earth!

The Soup's On Quilt was inspired by this group project by The Soup Kitchen. ▶

Each quilter made blocks with the general theme of "soup kitchen" with no size or color limitations. Fitting them all together was the fun challenge!

The Soup Kitchen members: Jackie Saling, Maggie Bullock, Cyndi Tobias, Lou McKee, Pam Mostek and Jean VanBockel

IMPORTED FROM
ITALY
OLIVE OIL
EXTRA LIGHT
NATURAL

Soup's On Wall Quilt

Soup's On Wall Quilt 45½" x 57½"	FIRST CUT	
	Number of Strips or Pieces	Dimensions
SOUP POT BLOCK		
Background ½ yard*	1	14½" x 6½"
	1	10½" x 2"
	1	10½" x 1"
	1	4" x 12½"
	1	1" x 1½"
Soup Pot ⅓ yard	1	10½" square
	1	1" x 11½"

Soup Ladle - ⅛ yard
Vegetable Appliqués - Assorted scraps
For directional fabric, the measurement that is listed first runs parallel to selvage (strip width).

FRUIT BOWL BLOCK		
Background ¼ yard	1	5½" x 9½"
	2	1½" x 8½"
	2	1½" squares
Fruit Bowl ⅙ yard	1	4" x 7½"
	1	1½" x 7½"
	2	1½" x 3"
Fruit Bowl Accent Scrap	1	1½" x 7½"
Raspberry Basket Scrap	1	2¾" x 5½"
Basket Trim Scrap	1	¾" x 5½"

Plum and Raspberry Appliqués - Assorted scraps

FLOUR AND BREAD BLOCK		
Background ⅛ yard	1	2½" x 9½"
	2	2½" x 8½"
	1	1½" x 9½"
Flour Bag ¼ yard	1	8" x 9½" (trimmed to 5½" x 8½")
	2	1½" squares

Bread Appliqués - Assorted scraps
Embroidery Thread - Red & Black

SOUP'S ON BLOCK		
Background ¼ yard	1	6½" x 14"
Borders ⅛ yard	2	2" x 14"

Lettering Appliqués - ⅛ yard
Small Pea and Tomato Appliqués - Assorted scraps

Soup's On Wall Quilt continued	FIRST CUT	
	Number of Strips or Pieces	Dimensions
MENU BLOCK		
Background ¼ yard	1	9" x 12" (trimmed to 7½" x 10½")
Border ⅛ yard	2	1½" x 10½"
	2	1½" x 7½"
Corners Scrap	4	1½" squares

Chili Appliqués - Assorted scraps
Embroidery Thread - Black

DIAMOND BLOCKS (Make 3)		
Background Triangles *Cut for each block*	4	2¾" squares (one color for each block)
Center Triangles *Cut assorted colors for each block*	4	2¾" squares (in assorted colors)

NINE-PATCH BLOCKS (Make 2)		
Corner *Cut for each block*	4	2" squares
Cross *Cut for each block*	4	2" squares
Center *Cut for each block*	1	2" square

SHOO FLY BLOCKS (Make 2)		
Corner *Cut for each block*	4	2" squares
Cross and Outside Triangles *Cut for each block*	8	2" squares
Center *Cut for each block*	1	2" square

Soup's On Wall Quilt continued	FIRST CUT	
	Number of Strips or Pieces	Dimensions
MIXED VEGETABLE BLOCK		
Background ¼ yard	1	7" x 14"
	2	3" squares
	2	3" x 1½"
	2	1½" x 6"
Colander ¼ yard	1	5" x 12"
	1	1½" x 7"
	2	1½" squares

Vegetable Appliqués - Assorted scraps

BACKGROUNDS FOR VEGETABLE APPLIQUÉ BLOCKS		
Eggplant ¼ yard	1	5" x 9½"
Squash ⅙ yard	1	4½" x 9½"
Corn ¼ yard	1	7½" x 9½"
Chili Scrap	1	5" square
Onion Scrap	1	5" square
Asparagus ⅓ yard	1	8½" x 9½"
Peppers ⅓ yard	1	9" x 9½"
Peas ¼ yard	1	5" x 9½"

Vegetable Appliqués - Assorted scraps

BORDERS		
First Border Light Checks ¼ yard	3	2" x 42"
First Border Dark Checks ¼ yard	3	2" x 42"
Second Border ⅓ yard	5	1½" x 42"
Outside Border ⅔ yard	5	4½" x 42"
Binding ⅝ yard	6	2¾" x 42"

Lightweight Fusible Web - 1½ yards
Heavyweight Fusible Web - ¼ yard
Backing - 3 yards
Batting - 52" x 63"

Cutting Instructions

Read all instructions before beginning and use ¼"-wide seam allowances throughout. Read Cutting Strips and Pieces on page 108 prior to cutting fabrics.

Getting Started

This quilt includes fourteen appliqué blocks in varying sizes, each featuring a different fruit, vegetable, or other food-related motif. Some blocks include piecing and embroidery, and some are framed with borders. The quilt also includes a total of seven blocks in three traditional pieced patterns: Diamond, Nine-Patch, and Shoo Fly. Refer to Accurate Seam Allowance on page 108. Whenever possible, use the Assembly Line Method on page 108. Press seams in direction of arrows.

To keep construction simple, you'll find yardages, block layouts, and specific step-by-step instructions listed separately for each block. Information common to all blocks appears in Making the Blocks.

Preparing Embroidered Pieces

The Flour and Bread Block and Menu Block are embroidered. We scanned and digitized the embroidery patterns on pages 33 and 37 using Bernina® artista Embroidery Software and the Outline Stem Stitch. If you prefer hand embroidery, refer to Embroidery Stitch Guide on page 111 and use three strands of embroidery floss and a stem stitch. After pieces are embroidered, trim as indicated in cutting chart, making sure to allow room for appliqués.

Making the Blocks

Refer to appliqué instructions on page 109. Our instructions are for Quick-Fuse Appliqué. If you prefer hand appliqué, reverse templates, and add ¼"-wide seam allowances.

Refer to individual patterns for required number of regular and reverse appliqué pieces to cut for each block. Photo on page 28, layout below, and individual block diagrams show placement for appliqués and embroidery.

Use lightweight fusible web for all appliqués with the exception of the small tomato and all peas which use heavyweight. Finish appliqué edges with machine satin stitch or decorative stitching as desired, unless fused with heavyweight web.

Soup's On Wall Quilt
Finished size: 45½" × 57½"
Photo: page 28

Soup Pot Block

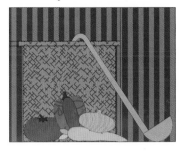

1. Sew 10½" Soup Pot square between 10½" × 2" and 10½" × 1" Background pieces as shown. Press.

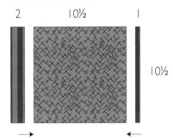

2. Sew 1" × 1½" Background piece to 1" × 11½" Soup Pot piece as shown. Press. Sew this unit between 4" × 12½" Background piece and unit from step 1. Press. Sew unit to 14½" × 6½" Background strip. Press. Soup Pot Block measures 18½" × 14½".

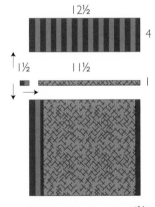

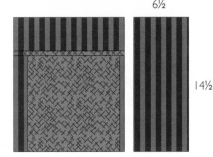

Block Measures 18½ x 14½

Fruit Bowl Block

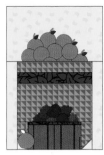

1. Sew 1½" × 7½" Fruit Bowl Accent piece between 1½" × 7½" and 4" × 7½" Fruit Bowl pieces. Press.

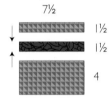

2. Refer to Quick Corner Triangles on page 108. Sew 1½" Background square to one 1½" × 3" Fruit Bowl piece as shown. Press. Make two, one of each variation.

Background = 1½ × 1½
Fruit Bowl = 1½ × 3
Make 2
(1 of each variation)

3. Sew ¾" × 5½" Basket Trim piece to 2¾" × 5½" Raspberry Basket piece as shown. Press. Sew this unit between units from step 2. Press.

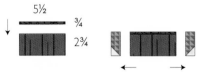

4. Refer to Quick Fuse Appliqué on page 109. Trace seven Raspberry Patterns on page 38. Cut appliqués from assorted scraps.

5. Referring to photo on page 28, block layout, and diagram in step 6, position and fuse raspberry appliqués on unit from step 1, allowing bottom edges of appliqués to overhang bottom edge of unit slightly. Carefully trim appliqué overhang even with unit. Finish appliqué edges as desired.

6. Sew unit from step 3 to unit from step 5 as shown. Press. Sew unit between two 1½" × 8½" Background pieces. Press.

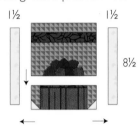

7. Trace eleven Plum, five stem and leaf patterns on page 38. Cut appliqués from assorted scraps. Set one plum, stem, and leaf aside. These will be added later. Referring to photo on page 35, block layout, and diagram in step 8, position and fuse ten plum and four stem and leaf appliqués on 5½" × 9½" Background piece, allowing bottom edges of appliqués to overhang bottom edge of background slightly. Carefully trim appliqué overhang even with background. Finish appliqué edges as desired.

8. Sew unit from step 7 to unit from step 6. Press. Fruit Bowl Block measures 9½" × 13½".

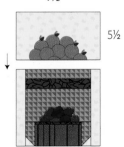

Block Measures 9½ x 13½

Flour and Bread Block

1. Refer to Quick Corner Triangles on page 108. Sew one 1½" Flour Bag square to one 2½" × 8½" Background piece as shown. Press. Make two, one of each variation.

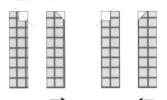

Flour Bag = 1½ × 1½
Background = 2½ × 8½
Make 2
(1 of each variation)

2. Sew embroidered 5½" × 8½" Flour Bag piece between units from step 1 as shown. Press. Sew 1½" × 9½" Background piece to top of unit. Press. Unit measures 9½" square. Remaining Background and Bread will be added in Assembly.

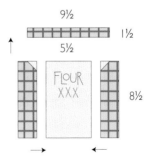

Unit Measures 9½" square

Soup's On Block

1. Sew 6½" × 14" Background strip between two 2" × 14" Border strips as shown. Press.

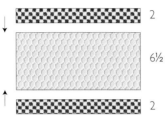

Block measures 14" × 9½"

2. Trace lettering, small pea, and small tomato patterns on page 38. Refer to Quick Fuse Appliqué on page 109. Use lightweight fusible web for lettering and heavyweight for small tomato and pea. Cut one of each piece from assorted scraps.

3. Referring to photo on page 28 and block layout, position and fuse appliqués on unit from step 1 as shown. Finish lettering appliqué edges as desired. Soup's On Block measures 14" × 9½".

Menu Block

1. Sew one 1½" × 7½" Border piece between two 1½" Corner squares as shown. Press. Make two.

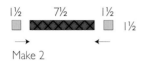

Make 2

2. Sew embroidered 7½" × 10½" Background piece between two 1½" × 10½" Border pieces as shown. Press. Sew this unit between two units from step 1. Press. Menu Block measures 9½" × 12½".

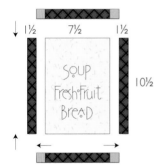

Block Measures 9½" × 12½"

3. Refer to Quick Fuse Appliqué on page 109. Trace Chili pattern on page 40. Cut one and one reversed from scraps. Referring to photo on page 28 and block layout, position and fuse appliqués on unit from step 2 as shown. Finish appliqué edges as desired.

Flour Embroidery Pattern

Diamond Blocks

You will be making three Diamond Blocks.

1. Sew two assorted 2¾" Center Triangle squares together as shown. Press. Make six. Sew two units together. Press. Make three in assorted colors.

2¾ 2¾

2¾

Make 6
in assorted colors

Make 3
in assorted colors

2. Refer to Quick Corner Triangles on page 108. Sew two matching 2¾" Background Triangle squares to opposite corners of each unit from step 1. Press. Sew two matching 2¾" Background squares to remaining corners of each unit. Press. Make three in assorted colors. Diamond Blocks measure 5" square.

Background Triangles = 2¾ x 2¾
Unit from step 1
Make 3 in assorted colors

Blocks measure 5" square

Nine-Patch and Shoo Fly Blocks

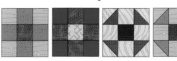

Make four nine-patch units. Two will be used as Nine-Patch Blocks. The remaining two units are used to construct two Shoo Fly Blocks.

1. Sew one 2" Cross square between two matching 2" Corner squares as shown. Press. Make eight, two of each color combination.

2   2   2

2

Make 8
(2 of each color combination)

2. Sew one 2" Center square between two matching 2" Cross squares as shown. Press. Make four, one of each color combination.

2   2   2

2

Make 4
(1 of each color combination)

3. Sew one unit from step 2 between matching units from step 1 as shown. Press. Make four blocks, one of each color combination. Set aside two Nine-Patch Blocks. Nine-Patch Blocks measure 5" square.

Make 4
(1 of each color combination)

Blocks measure 5" square
(2 for Nine-Patch, 2 for Shoo Fly)

4. Refer to Quick Corner Triangles on page 108. Sew matching 2" Outside Triangle squares to each remaining nine-patch unit from step 3 as shown. Press. Shoo Fly Blocks measure 5" square.

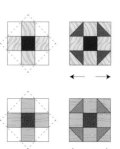

Outside Triangles = 2 x 2
Unit from step 3
Block measures 5" square

Mixed Vegetable Block

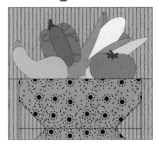

1. Refer to Quick Corner Triangles on page 108. Sew two 3" Background squares to 5" × 12" Colander piece as shown. Press.

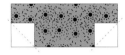

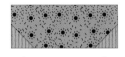

Background = 3 × 3
Colander = 5 × 12

2. Making a quick corner triangle unit, sew one 1½" Colander square to one 3" × 1½" Background piece as shown. Press. Make two, one of each variation.

Colander = 1½ × 1½
Background = 3 × 1½
Make 2
(1 of each variation)

3. Sew 1½" × 7" Colander piece between units from step 2 as shown. Press.

4. Sew unit from step 1 to unit from step 3 as shown. Press. Sew this unit between two 1½" × 6" Background pieces as shown. Press.

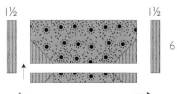

6

5. Refer to Quick Fuse Appliqué on page 109. Trace Corn, Pepper, Carrot, and Tomato Patterns on pages 38-40. Trace one reversed Squash/Eggplant pattern. Cut one of each piece from assorted scraps.

6. Referring to photo on page 28, block layout, and colander unit, position and fuse appliqués on 7" × 14" Background piece, aligning bottom edges of appliqué pieces with bottom edges of Background strip. Finish appliqué edges as desired.

7. Sew unit from step 6 to top of unit from step 4. Press seam toward colander. Mixed Vegetable Block measures 14" × 12½".

Vegetable Appliqué Blocks

1. Refer to Quick Fuse Appliqué on page 109. Use lightweight fusible web for all vegetables except peas. Use heavyweight fusible for peas. Trace Squash/Eggplant, Corn, Chili, Onion, Asparagus, Pepper, and Pea Patterns on pages 39-40. Cut required number of each piece from assorted scraps.

2. Refer to Cutting Chart, photo on page 28, and diagrams in Sections 1, 2, 3, 4, and 6 on page 36. Position and fuse appliqués on appropriate Vegetable Appliqué Background Blocks. Finish appliqué edges (except peas), and add indentation lines to squash, if desired.

M-m-m-m-m! You can almost smell the soup simmering on the stove! Dress up your kitchen with this cheerful, food-themed wall quilt, laden with all the ingredients for a favorite family-style meal. Whether the menu calls for a refreshing gazpacho or a hot-and-hearty minestrone, both the meal—and the décor— are guaranteed to garner year-round raves.

Assembly

1. **Section 1:** Arrange and sew 4½" × 9½" Squash block, Flour and Bread unit, and Fruit Bowl Block as shown. Press. Sew Soup Pot Block to top edge of this unit to complete Section 1. Press.

2. Trace Tomato, Pepper, Carrot, Onion, Soup Ladle, and Ladle Handle Patterns on pages 38-39. Cut required number of each piece from assorted scraps. Press 11" × 15" lightweight fusible web to Soup Ladle fabric scrap. Cut ½" × 14" strip. Referring to block layout on page 32, position and fuse appliqués and prepared strip on to Section 1. Finish appliqué edges as desired.

3. **Section 2:** Arrange and sew two Diamond Blocks, one Shoo Fly Block, and one Nine-Patch Block together as shown. Press. Sew unit to 5" × 9½" Eggplant block. Press. Sew Soup's On Block to bottom edge of this unit to complete Section 2. Press.

4. **Section 3:** Sew 2½" × 9½" Flour and Bread Background piece to 7½" × 9½" Corn Block as shown. Press. Sew 5" square Chili Block to 5" square Onion Block. Press. Sew units together to complete Section 3. Press.

5. Referring to photo on page 28 and layout on page 31, sew Section 2 to Section 3. Press. Sew Section 2/3 to Section 1. Press.

6. **Section 4:** Sew Menu Block to 5" × 9½" Peas Block as shown to complete Section 4. Press.

7. **Section 5:** Arrange and sew one Nine-Patch Block, one Diamond Block, and one Shoo Fly Block as shown. Press. Sew unit to Mixed Vegetable Block to complete Section 5. Press.

8. **Section 6:** Sew 8½" × 9½" Asparagus Block to 9" × 9½" Pepper Block as shown to complete Section 6. Press.

9. Sew Section 5 between Section 4 and Section 6. Press.

10. Sew unit from step 5 to unit from step 9. Press.

11. Refer to Quick-Fuse Appliqué on page 109. Trace French Bread Pattern on page 40. Cut pieces from assorted scraps. Referring to photo on page 28 and layout on page 31, position and fuse Bread appliqués on Flour and Bread Block. Position and fuse remaining plum, stem, and leaf appliqués to Fruit Bowl Block. Finish appliqué edges as desired.

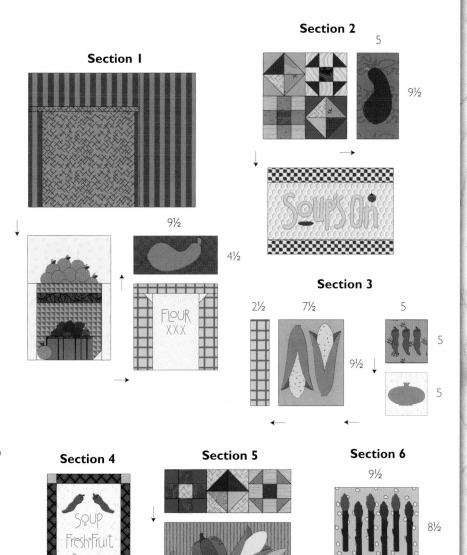

Borders

1. Sew three 2" × 42" First Border Light strips and three 2" × 42" First Border Dark strips together, alternating as shown, to make a strip set. Press.

2. Cut strip set into eighteen segments, each 2" wide. Sew five segments together as shown. Press. Make two and label them Side Borders. Sew four segments together. Press. Make two and label them Top and Bottom Borders.

Cut 18 segments

Make 2 strip sets with 5 segments (for side borders)
Make 2 strip sets with 4 segments (for top and bottom borders)

3. Use your seam ripper to carefully remove one dark square from end of each Side Border strip. Referring to photo on page 28 and layout on page 31, sew strips to sides of quilt. Press seams toward borders. Carefully remove one light square from end of each Top and Bottom Border strip. Sew strips to top and bottom of quilt. Press.

4. Sew 1½" × 42" Second Border strips end-to-end to make one continuous 1½"-wide strip. Press. Refer to Adding the Borders on page 110. Measure quilt through center from side to side. Cut two 1½"-wide Second Border strips to that measurement. Sew to top and bottom of quilt. Press seams toward Second Border strips.

5. Measure quilt through center from top to bottom, including borders just added. Cut two 1½"-wide Second Border strips to that measurement. Sew to sides of quilt. Press.

6. Refer to steps 4 and 5 to join, measure, trim, and sew 4½"-wide Outside Border strips to top, bottom, and sides of quilt. Press seams toward borders.

Layering and Finishing

1. Cut backing crosswise into two equal pieces. Sew pieces together to make one 54" × 80" (approximate) Backing piece. Press and trim to 54" × 65".

2. Arrange and baste backing, batting, and top together, referring to Layering the Quilt on page 110. Hand or machine quilt as desired.

3. Sew 2¾" × 42" binding strips end-to-end to make one continuous 2¾"-wide strip. Refer to Binding the Quilt on page 111 and bind quilt to finish.

Menu Block Embroidery Pattern

Refer to photo on page 28 to adjust spacing.

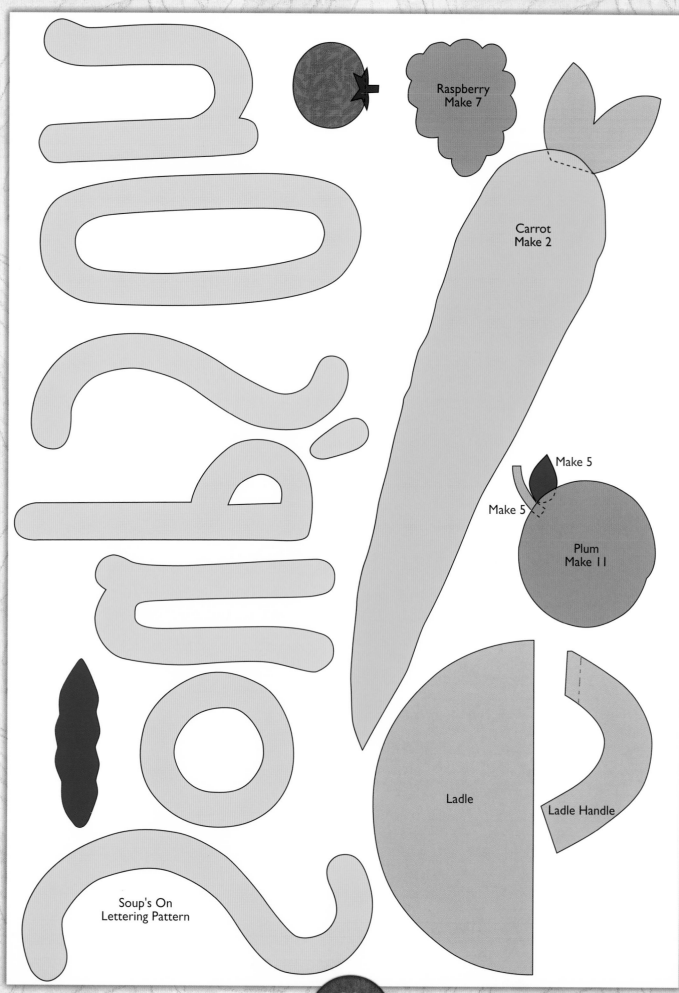

Raspberry
Make 7

Carrot
Make 2

Make 5

Make 5

Plum
Make 11

Ladle

Ladle Handle

Soup's On
Lettering Pattern

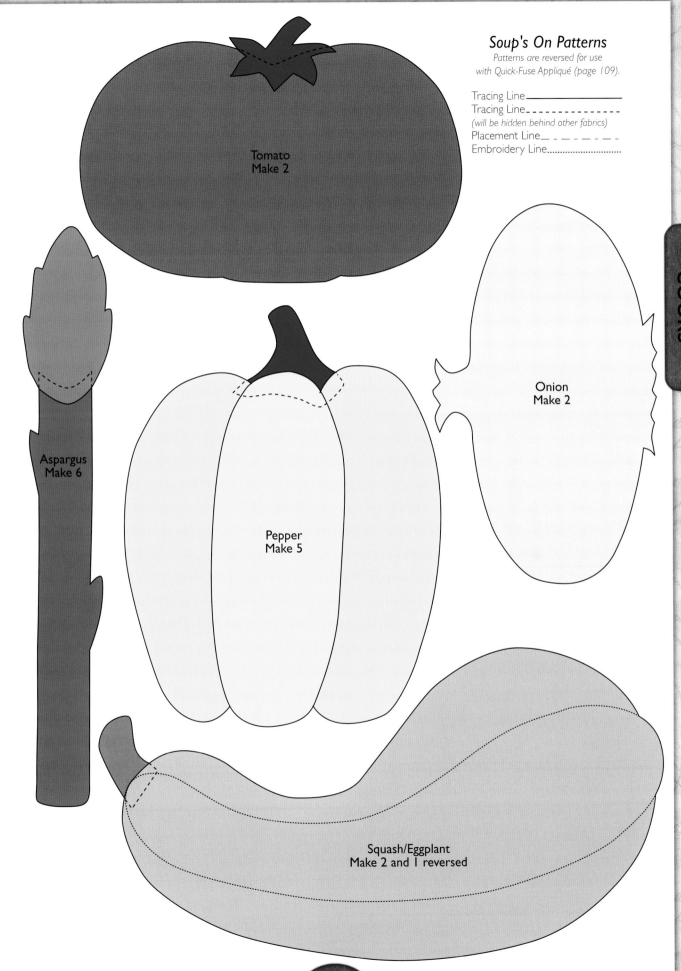

Tomato
Make 2

Soup's On Patterns
Patterns are reversed for use with Quick-Fuse Appliqué (page 109).

Tracing Line _____
Tracing Line - - - - - - - - - - - -
(will be hidden behind other fabrics)
Placement Line _ _ _ _ _ _ _
Embroidery Line ....

Onion
Make 2

Aspargus
Make 6

Pepper
Make 5

Squash/Eggplant
Make 2 and 1 reversed

creative woman
COOKS

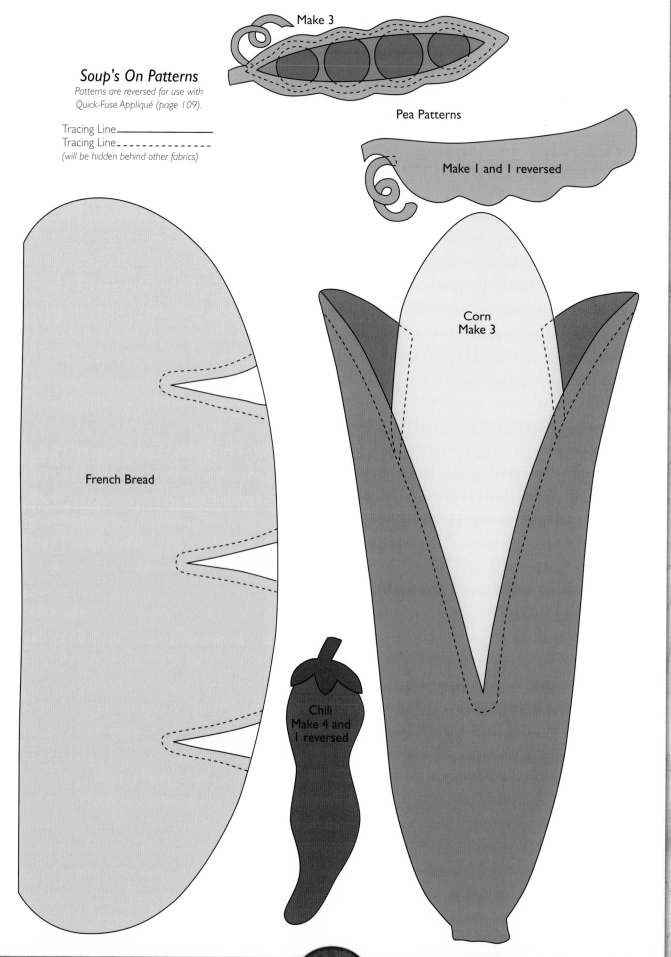

Soup's On Patterns

Patterns are reversed for use with Quick-Fuse Appliqué (page 109).

Tracing Line —————————
Tracing Line ---------------
(will be hidden behind other fabrics)

Make 3

Pea Patterns

Make 1 and 1 reversed

Corn
Make 3

French Bread

Chili
Make 4 and
1 reversed

Red Hot Apron

*Some like it hot! Spice up a plain purchased apron with this red hot design!
Use machine embroidery for the words and chili peppers, or embroider by
hand and add appliqués. Checked accents add to the kitchen couture.*

Getting Started

To add zing to a purchased apron, stitch on some fabric accents and embroidery. There are three options to embellish the apron: digitize and embroider the words and chilies, hand embroider, or embroider the words and appliqué the chilies.

Materials Needed

Purchased Apron

Accent Borders - ¼ yard

Embroidery Thread or Floss - Black, red, and green

(For appliquéd chilies, use red and green fabric scraps in place of embroidery thread and ⅛ yard lightweight fusible web.)

Embellishing the Apron

1. Cut two fabric strips for the accents. Measure the width along top edge of apron and the width 1½" below this edge. If the measurements differ, cut fabric strip 2" by the width of the larger measurement plus 1". Measure 10" below top edge of apron. Cut a second fabric strip 3½" by this width plus 1".

2. Press both long edges of each strip under ¼".

3. Place strips on front of apron as shown. Pin in place along long edges. Turn under short edges to match sides of apron and pin in place. Trim as needed.

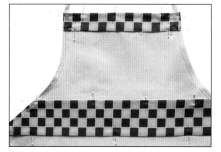

4. Sew fabric strips to apron by stitching close to all edges, pivoting at corners.

5. Referring to photo, Chili Pattern on page 40, and "Red Hot" lettering below, scan chili and word images. Using Bernina® artista embroidery software, digitize lettering using a Zigzag Outline Stitch and the chili using a Step Fill Stitch. Machine embroider. Or, refer to Embroidery Stitch Guide on page 111, use three strands of embroidery floss, and a satin stitch to embroider "Red Hot" and three chilies. To appliqué chilies, refer to Quick-Fuse Appliqué on page 109.

*Red Hot
Embroidery Pattern*

Fresh Salsa Table Topper

Finished size: 42½" x 42½"

Bring spice to your table with this red-hot topper, garnished with zesty appliqués. We used quick-and-easy methods for both piecing and appliqué, so you can cook up your version in no time flat. Add a basket of chips, your homemade salsa, and a cool beverage of your choice–the results are "instant fiesta!"

Cutting Instructions

Read all instructions before beginning and use ¼"-wide seam allowances throughout. Read Cutting Strips and Pieces on page 108 prior to cutting fabrics.

Getting Started

This table topper features a center block surrounded by a series of borders in varying fabrics and widths. Refer to Accurate Seam Allowance on page 108. Whenever possible, use the Assembly Line Method on page 108. Press seams in direction of arrows.

The appliqués are added with fusible web and finished with decorative machine stitching. The backing is sewn right sides together with the top and turned; there is no batting or binding. We stitched-in-the-ditch in a few key seams to hold the two layers together.

Assembly

1. Sew one 5" Fabric B square between two 5" Fabric A squares as shown. Press. Make two.

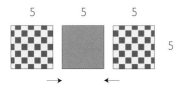

Make 2

Fresh Salsa Table Topper 42½" x 42½"	FIRST CUT	
	Number of Strips or Pieces	Dimensions
Fabric A *Nine-Patch Block Squares & Outside Border* 1⅛ yards	5	5½" x 42" "Fussy Cut" border
	4	5" squares
Fabric B *Nine-Patch Block Squares* ¼ yard	4	5" squares
Fabric C *First Border & Patchwork Block Corners* ½ yard	4 20	5" x 14 2¾" squares
Fabric D *Patchwork Blocks* ¼ yard	1 8	5" square 2¾" squares
Fabric E *Patchwork Blocks* ⅛ yard	8	2¾" squares

Fresh Salsa Table Topper continued	FIRST CUT	
	Number of Strips or Pieces	Dimensions
BORDERS		
Second & Fourth Borders ½ yard	8	1½" x 42"
Third Border ½ yard	4	3½" x 42"

Backing - 1¼ yards* or 2⅜ yards
*must be 44"-wide or wider
Tomato Appliqués - ⅛ yard
Chili & Stem Appliqués - Assorted scraps
Lightweight Fusible Web - ¼ yard

2. Refer to Quick Corner Triangles on page 108. Sew two 2¾" Fabric C squares to opposite corners of 5" Fabric D square as shown. Press. Sew two 2¾" Fabric C squares to remaining corners. Press.

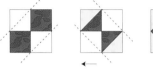

C= 2¾ x 2¾
D= 5 x 5

3. Sew unit from step 2 between two 5" Fabric B squares as shown. Press.

4. Sew together two 5" x 14" Fabric C strips, two units from step 1, and unit from step 3 as shown. Press.

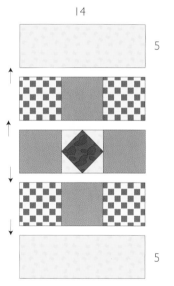

5. Sew 2¾" Fabric D squares and 2¾" Fabric E squares together in pairs as shown. Press. Make eight. Sew two units together. Press. Make four.

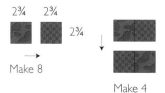

Make 8

Make 4

6. Making quick corner triangle units, sew two 2¾" Fabric C squares to opposite corners of each unit from step 5 as shown. Press. Sew two 2¾" Fabric C squares to remaining corners. Press. Make four.

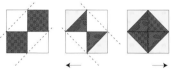

C= 2¾ x 2¾
Unit from step 5
Make 4

7. Sew one 5" x 14" Fabric C strip between two units from step 6 as shown, noting color placement. Press. Make two.

Make 2

8. Sew unit from step 4 between two units from step 7 as shown. Press.

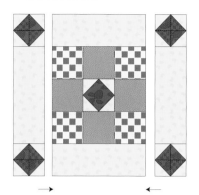

9. Refer to Adding the Borders on page 110. Measure quilt through center from side to side. Cut two 1½" x 42" Second Border strips to that measurement. Sew to top and bottom of quilt. Press seams toward Second Border.

Fresh Salsa Table Topper
Finished size: 42½" x 42½"
Photo: page 42

10. Measure quilt through center from top to bottom, including borders just added. Cut two 1½"-wide Second Border strips to that measurement. Sew to sides of quilt. Press.

11. Refer to steps 9 and 10 to measure, trim, and sew 3½"-wide Third Border strip and 1½"-wide Fourth Border strips to top, bottom, and sides of quilt. Press seams toward last border added.

12. Sew 5½" × 42" Outside Border strips end-to-end to make one continuous 5½"-wide strip. Repeat steps 9 and 10 to measure, trim, and sew Outside Border strips to top, bottom, and sides of quilt. Press.

Adding the Appliqués

Refer to appliqué instructions on page 109. Our instructions are for Quick-Fuse Appliqué, but if you prefer hand appliqué, add ¼"-wide seam allowances.

1. Trace Tomato and Chili Patterns on pages 39-40. Cut four tomatoes and four chilies from red scraps. Cut four tomato stems and four chili stems from green scraps.

2. Referring to photo on page 42 and layout on page 43, position and fuse appliqués. Finish edges with machine satin stitch or other decorative stitching as desired.

Layering and Finishing

1. Layer top and backing right sides together. Using ¼" seam, sew around edges leaving 6" opening for turning. Clip corners, turn, and press. Hand stitch opening closed.

2. Stitch-in-the-ditch around and through nine-patch center and along side of second and fourth borders to anchor top to backing, if desired.

---

creative concepts

Reversible Napkins

Finished size: 16" square

Take two fabrics, sew well, season with multi-colored buttons, and serve up a playful table! Reversible napkins add lots of decorating options, especially when they are all tied up with easy button napkin rings.

Materials Needed for Two Napkins

Fabric A - ½ yard
    Two 16½" squares
Fabric B - ½ yard
    Two 16½" squares

Making the Napkins

1. *Position and sew 16½" Fabric A and Fabric B squares, right sides together, using a ¼"-wide seam allowance and leaving a 4" opening for turning.*

2. *Clip corners and turn right side out. Press. Hand-stitch opening closed.*

3. *Edge-stitch or top-stitch close to edge of napkins.*

4. *Fold napkins so 1" of contrasting fabric shows.*

Button Napkin Rings

Cute and colorful napkin rings are a great finishing touch for a playful table setting. Simply sew buttons in various shapes and colors to grosgrain ribbon. We used seven buttons, alternating square and round shapes. Leave 6" of ribbon on each side of the buttons to tie into a square knot at the back of the napkin.

The Creative Woman By Debbie Mumm®

Decorated Kitchen Towels

Finished size: 20" x 28"

*Bright borders and red hot chili peppers add some zest to purchased towels.
Embroider or appliqué the chili peppers for a hot new look!*

Materials Needed

Two Kitchen Towels (20" x 28")

*Embroidery Thread - Red
and green*

Stabilizer

Towel A
*Fabric A (Solid) - ⅛ yard
One 1¼" x 21" strip*

*Fabric B (Checks) - ⅝ yard
One 3¼" x 21" bias-cut
strip*

Towel B
*Fabric A (Solid) - ¼ yard
One 4½" x 21" strip*

*Fabric B (Checks) - ⅛ yard
One 1¾" x 21" strip*

Making Towel A

1. Sew 1¼" x 21" Fabric A strip
to 3¼" x 21" Fabric B strip as
shown. Press.

Width of towel plus 1"

1¼

Bias cut

3¼

2. Turn 21"-long Fabric A edge
under ¼" and press.

3. Place right side of fabric strip on
wrong side of towel. Stitch along
bottom edge of Fabric B strip,
½" from edge of towel as shown.
Fold fabric away from towel and
press seam toward fabric.

Wrong side of towel

4. Referring to photo, turn
fabric to front of towel, tucking
side edge seam allowance under
fabric, flush with edge of towel.
Press and pin in place.

5. Stitch along side and top
edges of fabric, close to folded
edges, to attach to towel,
pivoting at corners.

6. Referring to photo and Chili
Pattern on page 40, scan chili
image. Digitize chili using
Bernina® artista Embroidery
Software and a step fill stitch.
Use stabilizer and red and green
embroidery threads to machine
embroider chilies. Or, refer to
Embroidery Stitch Guide on
page 111, use three strands of
embroidery floss, and a satin
stitch to embroider four chilies.

Making Towel B

1. Sew 1¾" x 21" Fabric B to
4½" x 21" Fabric A as shown.
Press.

Width of towel plus 1"

1¾

4½

2. Turn 21"-long edges under ¼"
and press. Referring to photo,
position and pin fabric strip to
front of towel. Turn side edges
under to match edge of towel,
tucking seam allowance
between fabric strip and towel.
Press and pin sides in place.

3. Stitch close to folded edge of
fabric to attach to towel.

4. Refer to step 6, Making
Towel A to embroider chilies.

A sense of humor... is needed armor. Joy in one's heart and some laughter on one's lips is a sign that the person down deep has a pretty good grasp of life.
~Hugh Sidey

The Creative Woman
Relaxes

Margie Karavitis

Bennett Cerf once said that a person who can bring the spirit of laughter into a room is indeed blessed. And award-winning quilter, Margie Karavitis, is certainly blessed. Margie loves to tell this story:

Several years ago, Margie was traveling to a quilt show and had to change planes. She had a lengthy layover and arrived at the gate very early, before anyone else was there. Always resourceful, Margie took a piece of appliqué out of her bag to work on and decided that her appliqué would look better if she used invisible thread. So, Margie sat, working away, for quite some time, oblivious to the fact that lots of people had arrived at the gate and the waiting area had gotten very crowded. When Margie finally looked up, she realized that all the seats were taken and people were standing...all the seats, that is, except those right around Margie. "I think they thought I was nuts," Margie says with a chuckle. "Since no one could see the invisible thread, they thought I was just stitching away with an empty needle!"

Detail of one of Margie's quilts

Margie always liked to sew, but didn't make her first quilt until she was fifty. Then she bought a kit from a department store because she needed a spread for her bed. Now, thirty years later, Margie specializes in piecing traditional patterns but loves to put a different spin on the ways they are quilted. What to do with a quilt after it's pieced is Margie's personal challenge. A challenge she has met with award-winning quilts, including two on permanent display at the American Quilter's Society Museum.

Everybody needs beauty as well as bread, places to play in and pray in, where nature may heal and give strength to body and soul. ~John Muir

47

Serenity Circles Quilt

Serenity Circles Quilt 48½" x 57½"	FIRST CUT	
	Number of Strips or Pieces	Dimensions
Fabric A *Background* 1½ yards	20	9½" squares
Fabric B *Light Quarter-Circle* 5/8 yard **each** of two fabrics	6* *Cut for each fabric*	9" squares
Fabric C *Medium Light Quarter-Circle* 7/8 yard	10	9" squares
Fabric D *Medium Quarter-Circle* 7/8 yard	10	9" squares
Fabric E *Dark Quarter-Circle* 7/8 yard	10	9" squares
BORDERS		
First Border ¼ yard	5	1¼" x 42"
Second Border ⅓ yard	5	1½" x 42"
Outside Border ¾ yard	5	4½" x 42"
Binding 5/8 yard	6	2¾" x 42"

Backing - 3⅛ yards
Batting - 55" x 64"

Cutting Instructions

Read all instructions before beginning and use ¼"-wide seam allowances throughout. Read Cutting Strips and Pieces on page 108 prior to cutting fabrics.

Getting Started

This quilt includes twenty 9½" square (unfinished) blocks. The block has a quarter-circle machine-appliquéd to each of its four corners. The same background fabric (Fabric A) and three of the four quarter-circle fabrics (Fabrics C, D, and E) are repeated in every block. Two slightly different fabrics (Fabric B) are used to make the quarter-circles for the remaining corner. This subtle variation in fabric adds an interesting twist to the simple design. Arrange the blocks as we have, or experiment to find your own perfect arrangement.

The quarter-circles are created by layering and stitching two matching pieces of fabric, cutting out a full circle, and then cutting the circle into fourths. The circles are turned and pressed, then stitched to the block corners with an invisible or blind-hem machine stitch. Hand appliqué or straight machine stitching may also be used.

Refer to Accurate Seam Allowance on page 108. Whenever possible, use the Assembly Line Method on page 108. Press seams in direction of arrows.

Serenity Circle Blocks

1. Use Serenity Circle quarter-circle pattern on page 52 to make full-circle template. Trace circle on wrong side of one 9" Fabric B square. Layer right sides together with matching 9" Fabric B square. Stitch on drawn line. Cut out circle, trimming seam allowance to 3/16". Make six circles, three from each Fabric B.

Fabric B
Make 6
(3 of each variation)

2. Cut each Fabric B circle into fourths as shown. Clip or notch curves, turn right side out, and press. You need ten quarter-circles of each Fabric B for this quilt. Set remaining quarter-circles aside for another project.

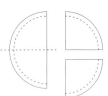 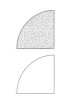

Cut in fourths   Make 10 sections of each Fabric B

3. Repeat steps 1 and 2 to make five circles each from Fabric C, Fabric D, and Fabric E. Cut each circle into fourths for a total of twenty quarter-circles in each fabric.

 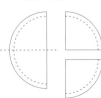

Fabric C = Make 5
Fabric D = Make 5   Cut in fourths
Fabric E = Make 5

Make 20 sections **each** of Fabrics C, D, and E

4. Position one quarter-circle each of Fabric B, Fabric C, Fabric D, and Fabric E on corners of one 9½" Fabric A square as shown. Use a machine blind-stitch and invisible thread to stitch curved edges of quarter-circles to block. Make twenty blocks total, ten with each Fabric B. Blocks measure 9½" square.

Make 20 (ten of each combination)
Blocks measure 9½" square

Assembly

1. Refer to photo on page 46 and layout. Arrange blocks in five horizontal rows of four blocks each as shown.

2. Sew blocks into rows. Press seams in opposite directions from row to row.

3. Sew rows together. Press.

4. Sew 1¼" × 42" First Border strips end-to-end to make one continuous 1¼"-wide strip. Press. Refer to Adding the Borders on page 110. Measure quilt through center from side to side. Cut two 1¼"-wide First Border strips to that measurement. Sew to top and bottom of quilt. Press seams toward border.

5. Measure quilt through center from top to bottom, including borders just added. Cut two 1¼"-wide First Border strips to that measurement. Sew to sides of quilt. Press.

6. Refer to steps 4 and 5 to join, measure, trim, and sew 1½"-wide Second Border strips and 4½"-wide Outside Border strips to top, bottom, and sides of quilt. Press seams toward newly added border strips.

Layering and Finishing

1. Cut backing crosswise into two equal pieces. Sew pieces together to make one 56" × 80" (approximate) backing piece. Press and trim to 56" × 64".

2. Arrange and baste backing, batting, and top together, referring to Layering the Quilt on page 110.

3. Hand or machine quilt as desired.

4. Sew 2¾" × 42" binding strips end-to-end to make one continuous 2¾"-wide strip. Refer to Binding the Quilt on page 110 and bind quilt to finish.

Serenity Circles Quilt
Finished size: 48½" × 57½"
Photo: page 46

Time Out for Tea Wall Quilt

Finished size: 36" x 33½"

Even the most dedicated creative woman needs a moment to pause, reflect, and "refuel." Whether you prefer a drowsy afternoon of daydreams and doodles, or a lively idea-swap with like-minded friends, this delightful wall quilt suits the occasion to a "tea!" The fresh yellow-and-blue palette hints at a country-cottage getaway, and the quick-fuse methods will have you relaxing in no time at all!

Cutting Instructions

Read all instructions before beginning and use ¼"-wide seam allowances throughout. Read Cutting Strips and Pieces on page 108 prior to cutting fabrics.

Getting Started

This quilt includes four 13½" x 12¼" blocks unfinished, each featuring a two-fabric, quick-fused teapot motif. For additional interest, we've chosen two fabrics in contrasting colors for the backgrounds, a snappy stripe for the First Border, and a directional fabric for the Outside Border. Refer to Accurate Seam Allowance on page 108.

Whenever possible, use the Assembly Line Method on page 108. Press seams in direction of arrows.

Teapot Blocks

Refer to appliqué instructions on page 109. Our instructions are for Quick-Fuse Appliqué. If you prefer hand appliqué, reverse templates as needed and add ¼"-wide seam allowances.

Note: Block backgrounds are not square. The 13½" edges are top and bottom measurements and 12¼" edges are side measurements.

1. Trace Teapot Center, Spout, Base, Handle, and Lid Patterns on page 51-52. Cut two Teapot Centers, one Spout, one Base, and one Handle from each of four teapot fabrics. Cut two Teapot Centers and one Lid from each remaining teapot fabric.

Time Out for Tea Wall Quilt 36" x 33½"	FIRST CUT	
	Number of Strips or Pieces	Dimensions
Fabric A Background ½ yard **each** of two fabrics	2*	13½" x 12¼"
	*Cut for each fabric	
BORDERS		
First Border ⅛ yard	2	1" x 26½"
	2	1" x 25"
Outside Border 1 yard** (directional) **OR** ⅝ yard (non-directional)	2**	33" x 4½"
	2	4½" x 27½"
	OR	
	4	4½" x 42"

Time Out for Tea Wall Quilt continued	FIRST CUT	
	Number of Strips or Pieces	Dimensions
Binding ⅜ yard	4	2¾" x 42"

Teapot Centers, Spout, Base, Handle, and Lid Appliqués - ⅛ yard *each* of eight fabrics
Backing - 1⅛ yards
Batting - 40" x 38"
Lightweight Fusible Web - ⅞ yard

**For directional fabric, the measurement that is listed first runs parallel to selvage (strip width).

The Creative Woman By Debbie Mumm®

2. Refer to photo and layout. Position and fuse appliqués on 13½" × 12¼" Fabric A pieces as shown. Stitch over butted edges of teapot center pieces with machine zigzag stitch, and finish remaining appliqué edges with satin stitch or decorative stitching as desired.

Assembly

1. Refer to photo and layout, arrange blocks in two horizontal rows of two blocks each as shown.

2. Sew blocks together. Press seams in opposite directions in each row.

3. Sew rows together. Press.

4. Sew 1" × 26½" First Border strips to top and bottom of quilt. Press seams toward border. Sew 1" × 25" First Border strips to sides. Press.

5. Sew 4½" × 27½" Outside Border strips to top and bottom of quilt. Press seams toward border. Sew 33" × 4½" Outside Border strips to sides. Press.

Layering and Finishing

1. Arrange and baste backing, batting, and top together, referring to Layering the Quilt on page 110.

2. Hand or machine quilt as desired.

3. Sew 2¾" × 42" binding strips end-to-end to make one continuous 2¾"-wide strip. Refer to Binding the Quilt on page 110 and bind quilt to finish.

Time Out for Tea Patterns
Patterns are reversed for use with Quick-Fuse Appliqué (page 109).

Tracing Line ——————
Tracing Line – – – – – – –
(will be hidden behind other fabrics)

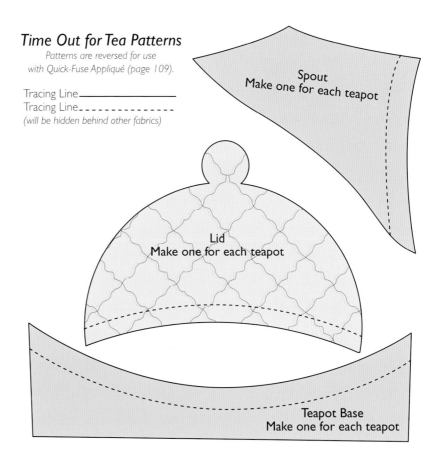

Time Out for Tea Wall Quilt
Finished size: 36" × 33½"
Photo: page 50

Handle
Make one for each teapot

Time Out for Tea Patterns

Tracing Line —————
Tracing Line - - - - - - - - - - -
(will be hidden behind other fabrics)
Placement Line — - — - — -

Center

Teapot Center
Make four
(two of each color) for each teapot

**Quarter-Circle for
Serenity Circles Quilt**

Trace Quarter-Circle Pattern
four times, aligning placement lines
to make an 8" circle.

creative concepts

Tea and Tales Tray

Instead of reading tea leaves, read your tea tray! Decorated with copies of hand-written journal notes and illustrations, this tea tray is perfect to use in your cozy reading corner.

Materials Needed

Unfinished Wood Tray
Decoupage Medium
Acrylic Craft Paint - Medium/Dark blue
   and black
Assorted Paintbrushes
Copies of Pages of Copyright-Free
   Book, Journal, or Scrapbook Paper
Sandpaper
Water-Based Burnt Umber Glaze

We used copies of an artist's journal pages, with her permission, for our tray, but you could also use sheet music, children's book pages, or pages from an illustrated book. Just make sure that any copied material is copyright-free.

Making the Tray

1. Sand tray to prepare for painting.

2. Paint tray with medium/dark blue paint. When thoroughly dry, sand edges to distress. Spray with matte varnish.

3. Referring to Relaxing Reading Lamp, page 53, Making the Lamp Base, step 3, spatter tray with black paint. Allow to dry.

4. Roughly tear elements from paper copies and attach to tray following directions on decoupage medium. When dry, apply several more coats of decoupage medium. Allow to dry.

5. Following manufacturer's directions, apply burnt umber glaze to entire tray, leaving glaze heavier on outside edges of decoupage area. When thoroughly dry, spray with matte varnish.

The Creative Woman By Debbie Mumm®

Relaxing Reading Lamp

You'll be ready to relax, curled up with a good book and cozy under your quilt, with this pretty lamp to light your way.

Materials Needed

Purchased Wooden Lamp

Acrylic Craft Paints - Light blue, medium blue, gold, black

Paintbrushes and Old Toothbrush

Sea Sponge

Water-Based Burnt Umber Glaze

Matte Spray Varnish

Fine Sandpaper

Scotch™ Magic™ Tape

Self-Adhesive Lampshade

Fabric - ⅝ yard directional or refer to manufacturer's directions on lampshade

Decorative Trim - 1½ yards

Fabric Glue

Making the Lamp Base

1. Lightly sand lamp base to remove gloss. Using features of lamp as a guide, determine where to paint each color, leaving several sections natural. Allow paint to dry thoroughly between each step.

2. Use Scotch™ Magic™ Tape to mask off natural-colored areas. Paint base and blue sections of lamp with light blue paint and allow to dry. Place small amount of medium blue paint on plastic plate or palette. Wet sea sponge with water and wring thoroughly. Dip sponge in medium blue paint; blot by tapping on a paper towel several times. Using a tapping motion, sponge paint over light blue paint. Use a light touch to achieve stipple effect. Referring to photo, apply more medium blue paint toward outside of lamp base. Allow to dry. Paint desired areas with gold paint. Allow to dry. Spray lamp base with matte varnish.

3. Mix black paint with a few drops of water and fill an old toothbrush with mixture. Rub thumb over bristles to add black spatters to entire lamp base. Practice on a piece of paper before applying to lamp. If spatters are too heavy, remove immediately using a cotton swab. Allow to dry. Apply burnt umber glaze to entire lamp base following manufacturer's directions. Allow to dry. Spray lamp base with one to two coats of matte varnish to finish.

Making the Shade

Note: If fabric is non-directional, follow directions included with lampshade.

1. Trace one side of lampshade to make pattern. Add ½" on all sides of traced pattern to make template. Referring to photo and fabric design, use template to cut four pieces of fabric.

2. Remove paper cover from self-adhesive shade. Place fabric on two opposite sides of shade, allowing ½"-wide margin of fabric to extend past lampshade edges. Smooth fabric to adhere.

3. Referring to step 2, cover remaining two sides of shade with fabric pieces. Turn under excess fabric at side edges and glue in place. Turn fabric at top and bottom to inside of shade and glue in place.

4. Glue decorative trim to bottom of shade, placing seam in an inconspicuous spot.

Stitches

Monique Scritchfield talking about her Mother, Marga House:

"The creative woman in my life knitted a sweater in less than 24 hours for a teenage daughter going to a special dance; figured out how to stretch a 16 oz. steak to feed seven; made all of her own, and six children's clothes; created a cozy home with her own blood, sweat, and tears (not always in that order); and just a few years ago, made sure that all nine of her grandchildren had quilts 'made by Grandma.'

As a teenager, when it seemed that we had nothing else in common, she and I always shared our love for sewing and crafts. It was the glue that held us together through tumultuous times, the conversation on the phone when there was nothing else to talk about. Now, the love of sewing, quilting, knitting, cross-stitch, needlepoint, and crafts is something that we share over the miles; it fuels the desire to be closer to each other and the gleam in our eyes as we create something that we just 'know' the other one is going to love!"

Monique Scritchfield and Marga House

Hand-quilting completed this future heirloom, stitched lovingly by friends.

This friendship quilt celebrates the birth of a special baby. Whimsical animals were embroidered on odd-sized blocks by each of the friends. The blocks were sewn together in a random pattern so animals are every-which-way.

Heather and Joe Butler proudly show off Baby Miles' Quilt

Whimsical Stitches Lap Quilt

Whimsical Stitches Lap Quilt 43" × 59"	FIRST CUT		SECOND CUT	
	Number of Strips or Pieces	Dimensions	Number of Pieces	Dimensions
Fabric A *Background and Star Centers* 1⅛ yard	4	4½" × 42"	12 / 26	4½" squares / 4½" × 2½"
	4	2½" × 42"		
	4	1½" × 42"	20 / 64	1½" × 2½" / 1½" squares
Fabric B *Block Corners* ¼ yard	2	2½" × 42"		
Fabric C *Inside Star Point and Block Corners* ½ yard	5	2½" × 42"	48	2½" squares
Fabric D *Outside Star Points* ½ yard	6	2½" × 42"	24 / 48	2½" × 4½" / 2½" squares
Fabric E *Pink Sashing* ⅛ yard	1	2½" × 42"	16 / 8	2½" × 1½" / 1½" squares
Fabric F *Green Sashing* ⅙ yard	1	2½" × 42"	8	2½" squares
	1	1½" × 42"	16	1½" squares
Fabric G *Orange Sashing* ⅛ yard	1	2½" × 42"	8	2½" squares
Fabric H *Yellow Sashing* ⅙ yard	1	4½" × 42"	7	4½" squares
BORDERS				
First Border ⅙ yard	4	1" × 42"		
Second Border ¼ yard	4	1½" × 42"		
Third Border ⅓ yard	5	2" × 42"		
Outside Border ¾ yard	5	4½" × 42"		
Binding ¼ yard each of four fabrics	2*	2¾" × 42" *Cut for each fabric	3**	2¾" × 18½" **Cut three for each of three fabrics and four of one fabric
OR ⅝ yard	6	2¾" × 42"		

Backing - 2¾ yards
Batting - 49" × 65"
Assorted Buttons - Six large 1"-1½"
Stabilizer - 1⅛ yards
Assorted Threads or Embroidery Floss - Rose, lime, orange, hot pink, purple

Cutting Instructions

Read all instructions before beginning and use ¼"-wide seam allowances throughout. Read Cutting Strips and Pieces on page 108 prior to cutting fabrics.

Getting Started

This quilt includes six Star Blocks set with two variations of pieced sashing to create a secondary block. Sashing is embellished with embroidery stitches. The quilt is finished with a four-color pieced binding. Refer to Accurate Seam Allowance on page 108. Whenever possible, use the Assembly Line Method on page 108. Press seams in direction of arrows. Star Block measures 12½" square unfinished.

Star Blocks

1. Sew 2½" × 42" Fabric B strip and 2½" × 42" Fabric A strip together as shown. Press. Make two. Cut strip sets into twenty-four 2½"-wide segments.

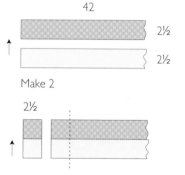

Make 2

Cut 24 segments

2. Sew 2½" × 42" Fabric A strip and 2½" × 42" Fabric C strip together. Press. Make two. Cut strip sets into twenty-four 2½"-wide segments.

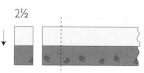

Cut 24 segments

3. Sew one segment from step 1 to one segment from step 2 as shown. Press. Make twenty-four.

Make 24

4. Refer to Quick Corner Triangles on page 108. Sew two 2½" Fabric D squares to one 4½" × 2½" Fabric A piece as shown. Press. Make twenty-four.

D = 2½ × 2½
A = 4½ × 2½
Make 24

5. Making quick corner triangle units, sew two 2½" Fabric C squares to one 2½" × 4½" Fabric D piece as shown. Press. Make twenty-four.

C = 2½ × 2½
D = 2½ × 4½
Make 24

6. Sew unit from step 4 to unit from step 5 as shown. Press. Make twenty-four.

Make 24

7. Sew one unit from step 6 between two units from step 3 as shown. Press. Make twelve.

Make 12

8. Sew one 4½" Fabric A square between two units from step 6 as shown. Press. Make six.

4½

4½

Make 6

9. Sew one unit from step 8 between two units from step 7 as shown. Press. Make six. Star Block measures 12½" square.

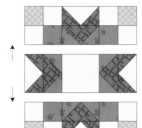

Make 6
Block measures 12½" square

Assembly

1. Refer to Quick Corner Triangles on page 108. Sew four 1½" Fabric A squares to one 2½" Fabric G square as shown. Press. Make eight.

A = 1½ × 1½
G = 2½ × 2½
Make 8

2. Sew one unit from step 1 between two 1½" × 2½" Fabric A pieces as shown. Press. Make eight.

1½   1½

   2½

Make 8

Whimsical Stitches Lap Quilt
(Decorative stitches and buttons not shown)
Finished size: 43" × 59"
Photo: page 54

3. Making quick corner triangles units, sew two 1½" Fabric A squares to one 2½" Fabric F square as shown. Press. Make eight.

A = 1½ x 1½
F = 2½ x 2½
Make 8

4. Making a quick corner triangle unit, sew 1½" Fabric A square to 2½" x 1½" Fabric E piece as shown. Press. Make sixteen, eight of each variation.

A = 1½ x 1½
E = 2½ x 1½
Make 16 (8 of each variation)

5. Sew unit from step 3 between one unit of each variation from step 4 as shown. Press. Make eight.

Make 8

6. Sew one unit from step 2 to one unit from step 5 as shown. Press. Make eight.

Make 8

7. Sew one 4½" Fabric H square between one 4½" Fabric A square and one unit from step 6 to make unit 1 as shown. Press. Make six. Sew one 4½" Fabric H square between two units from step 6, as shown, to make Unit 2. Press. Make one.

Unit 1   **Unit 2**
4½   4½

Make 6   Make 1

8. Making quick corner triangle units, sew two 1½" Fabric F squares to one 1½" x 2½" Fabric A piece as shown. Press. Make four.

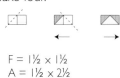

F = 1½ x 1½
A = 1½ x 2½
Make 4

9. Sew one unit from step 8 between two 1½" Fabric E squares as shown. Press. Make four.

1½   1½

  1½

Make 4

10. Making quick corner triangle units, sew four 1½" Fabric F squares to one 4½" x 2½" Fabric A piece as shown. Press. Make two.

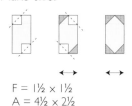

F = 1½ x 1½
A = 4½ x 2½
Make 2

11. Sew one unit from step 10 between two units from step 9 as shown. Press. Make two.

Make 2

This quilt draws its "whimsical" name from the rainbow of bright-and-breezy embroidery and button-bedecked blocks that give the quilt an intricate—but easy-to-stitch—overall design. Can you imagine a combination more likely to captivate the creative woman who loves to stitch?

12. Sew one unit from step 11 between two of Unit 1 from step 7 as shown. Press. Make two.

Make 2

13. Sew one Unit 1 from step 7 between two Star Blocks as shown. Press. Make two.

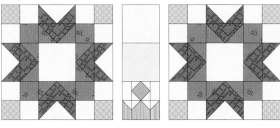

Make 2

14. Sew Unit 2 from step 7 between two Star Blocks as shown. Press.

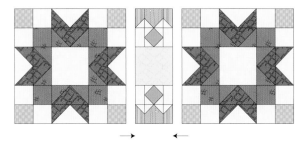

15. Referring to layout on page 57 and photo, arrange units from steps 12, 13, and 14. Sew rows together. Press.

Borders

1. Sew 1" × 42" First Border strips end-to-end to make one continuous 1"-wide strip. Press. Refer to Adding the Borders on page 110. Measure quilt through center from side to side. Cut two 1"-wide First Border strips to that measurement. Sew to top and bottom of quilt. Press seams toward border.

2. Measure quilt through center from top to bottom, including borders just added. Cut two 1"-wide First Border strips to that measurement. Sew to sides of quilt. Press.

3. Refer to steps 1 and 2 to join, measure, trim, and sew 1½"-wide Second Border, 2"-wide Third Border, and 4½"-wide Outside Border strips to top, bottom, and sides of quilt. Press.

Embroidery

1. Cut stabilizer into 5"-wide strips. Referring to photo, place stabilizer behind Star Block centers and sashing and follow manufacturer's instructions to stabilize areas for machine embroidery. If hand embroidery is desired, refer to Embroidery Stitch Guide on page 111.

2. Lightly mark a 2⅞" square in each stabilized Star Block center with a temporary fabric marker. Use purple thread to machine stitch a double-stitched blanket stitch on marked square as shown.

3. Use assorted-color threads to machine embroider decorative stitchery on sashing units. Mark placement lines with temporary marker. Suggested stitches include cross stitch, double cross stitch, double feather stitch, and Cretan. Remove all excess stabilizer.

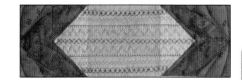

Layering and Finishing

1. Cut backing crosswise into two equal pieces. Sew pieces together to make one 49" × 80" (approximate) backing piece. Press and trim to 49" × 65".

2. Arrange and baste backing, batting, and top together, referring to Layering the Quilt on page 110. Hand or machine quilt as desired.

3. Referring to layout on page 57 and photo, sew 2¾" × 18½" assorted binding strips end-to-end to make one continuous 2¾"-wide strip. Refer to Binding the Quilt on page 110 and bind quilt to finish.

4. Refer to photo to sew button to center of each Star Block.

creative woman
STITCHES

I Love Purses Wallhanging

Finished size: 22" x 42"

Let's face it, lots of ladies love purses! Pay homage to your "passion for fashion"—and showcase your skill as a stitcher—with our lighthearted tribute to this indispensable accessory. Our quick-fused purses sport flaps, fringes, and other dimensional fripperies. Have fun choosing the just-right fabrics and eye-catching embellishments.

Cutting Instructions

Read all instructions before beginning and use ¼"-wide seam allowances throughout. Read Cutting Strips and Pieces on page 108 prior to cutting fabrics.

Getting Started

This quilt includes three purses that are quick-fuse appliquéd to a multi-bordered background block.

Two purses feature dimensional flaps that are layered and turned pillowslip-style. Interfacing is highly recommended and is included in the instructions. The finished flaps are tucked behind the base of the purse before the purse is fused to the background. Refer to appliqué instructions on page 109. Our instructions are for Quick-Fuse Appliqué. If you prefer hand appliqué, reverse templates and add ¼"-wide seam allowances.

Background Block

1. Sew 1½" x 13½" First Border strips to top and bottom of 13½" x 33½" Fabric A piece. Press seams toward borders. Sew 1½" x 35½" First Border strips to sides. Press.

2. Sew 1" x 15½" Second Border strips to top and bottom of unit from step 1. Press seams toward Second Border strips. Sew 1" x 36½" Second Border strips to sides. Press.

3. Sew 3" x 16½" Outside Border strips to top and bottom of unit from step 2. Press seams toward borders. Sew 3" x 41½" Outside Border strips to sides. Press.

I Love Purses Wallhanging 22" x 42"	FIRST CUT	
	Number of Strips or Pieces	Dimensions
Fabric A *Background* ½ yard	1	13½" x 33½"
BORDERS		
First Border ⅙ yard	2 / 2	1½" x 35½" / 1½" x 13½"
Second Border ⅛ yard	2 / 2	1" x 36½" / 1" x 15½"
Outside Border ⅓ yard	2 / 2	3" x 41½" / 3" x 16½"
Binding ⅝ yard for bias OR ⅜ yard for straight cuts	/ 4	2¾" Bias strips cut from 22" square OR 2¾" x 42"

I Love Purses Wallhanging continued		
Purse One - ¼ yard		
Purse One Flap and Lining - ⅛ yard		
Purse One Trim - Scrap		
Purse Two - ¼ yard		
Purse Three Flap and Lining - ⅛ yard		
Purse Three Top Section - ¼ yard		
Purse Three Base - Scrap		
Purse Three Handle - Scrap		
Backing - 1⅓ yards		
Batting - 26" x 46"		
Interfacing - ¼ yard		
Lightweight Fusible Web - ¾ yard		
Beaded Trims - ⅓ yard each of two trims		
Cord for Handles - ⅓ yard each of two cords		
One 1½" Button		

4. Using temporary fabric marker, mark purse placement lines. Referring to layout and measuring from lower Fabric A/ First Border seam line, mark placement lines at 2", 13", and 22" points at quilt center.

Purse One

1. Make template using Purse One Flap pattern on page 63. Layer Purse One Flap and Lining fabric right sides together over interfacing and trace flap onto fabric. Stitch on drawn lines, leaving top straight edge of flap open for turning. Cut out flap, ¼" away from stitched line and on drawn flap extension line. Clip corners and curves, turn right side out, and press.

Fold Line

2. Refer to Quick-Fuse Appliqué on page 109. Trace Purse Base and Purse Flap Trim patterns for Purse One on page 63. Cut appliqués from appropriate fabrics.

3. Refer to photo on page 60 and layout. Fuse Purse Flap Trim on Purse Flap as shown. Finish edges with a machine blanket stitch.

< Fold Line

4. Referring to photo on page 60 and layout, center Purse Base on quilt top, placing middle curve on 22" mark. With purse flap right side down, place flap extension under top edge of base as shown. Fuse Purse Base in place.

middle curve

5. Referring to photo on page 60 and layout, slip ends of 10" cord under top edge of Purse One Flap. Tack cording in place with matching-colored thread. Handle shape will be positioned after quilting. With flap open, finish edges of Purse Base with machine zigzag or decorative stitching as desired. Close flap.

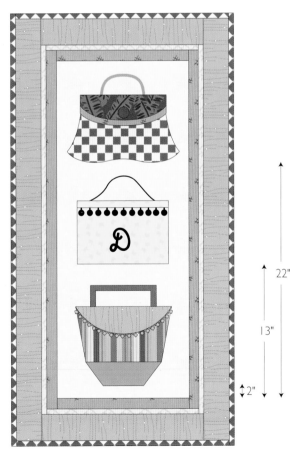

I Love Purses Wallhanging
Finished size: 22" × 42"
Photo: page 60

Purse Two

Purse Two features a monogram "D" for Debbie, of course! (D can also stand for Diva, Darling, or many other things.) If you wish, replace it with your own appliquéd or embroidered initial.

1. Refer to Quick-Fuse Appliqué on page 109. Draw 5½" × 9½" and ½" × 9½" rectangles on paper side of fusible web. Fuse to wrong side of Purse Two fabric and cut out. Referring to photo on page 60 and layout on page 61, center 5½" × 9½" Purse Two fabric piece on quilt top, placing bottom edge at 13" mark. Fuse in place.

2. Place beaded trim along top edge of Purse Two piece. Baste in place. Position ½" × 9½" Purse Two piece so it overlaps tape of trim.

   Tip: If tape of decorative trim is dark (ours is black), you may need to cover it with two fused ½" × 9½" layers of fabric.

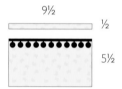

3. Refer to photo on page 60 and layout on page 61. Slip ends of cording under ½" × 9½" Purse Two piece. Fuse in place.

4. Trace "D" pattern for Purse Two on page 64. Cut appliqué from appropriate fabric. Fuse in place.

5. Finish outer edges of purse and "D" appliqué with machine zigzag or decorative stitching as desired.

Purse Three

1. Make template using Purse Three Flap pattern on page 64. Layer Purse Three Flap and Lining fabric right sides together over interfacing and trace flap onto fabric. Stitch on drawn lines, leaving top straight edge of flap open for turning. Cut out flap ¼" away from stitched line and on drawn flap extension line. Clip corners and curves, turn right side out and press.

Fold Line

2. Sew beaded trim to underside of Purse Three Flap curved edge.

3. Refer to Quick-Fuse Appliqué on page 109. Trace Top Section, Bottom Section, and Handle patterns for Purse Three on page 64. Cut appliqués from appropriate fabrics.

4. Refer to photo on page 60 and layout on page 61. Center Purse Three Top and Bottom Sections on quilt top placing lower edge of Bottom Section at 2" mark. With Purse Flap right side down, place flap extension under top edge of base as shown.

5. Fold flap down and insert Handle under straight edge, along top edge of purse. Fuse handle in place. Open flap and fuse purse. Close flap and finish Handle edge with machine zigzag or decorative stitching as desired. With flap open, finish edges of Top and Bottom Sections.

Layering and Finishing

1. Trim backing to 26" × 46". Arrange and baste backing, batting, and top together, referring to Layering the Quilt on page 110.

2. Hand or machine quilt as desired.

3. We used bias strips for our binding. Refer to Making Bias Strips on page 110. Approximately 130" of bias strips are needed. Sew 2¾" × 42" binding strips end-to-end to make one continuous 2¾"-wide strip. Refer to Binding the Quilt on page 110 and bind quilt to finish.

4. Refer to photo on page 60 and layout on page 61. Tack cord handles in place with matching thread. Sew large button to center of Purse One Flap through all layers of quilt.

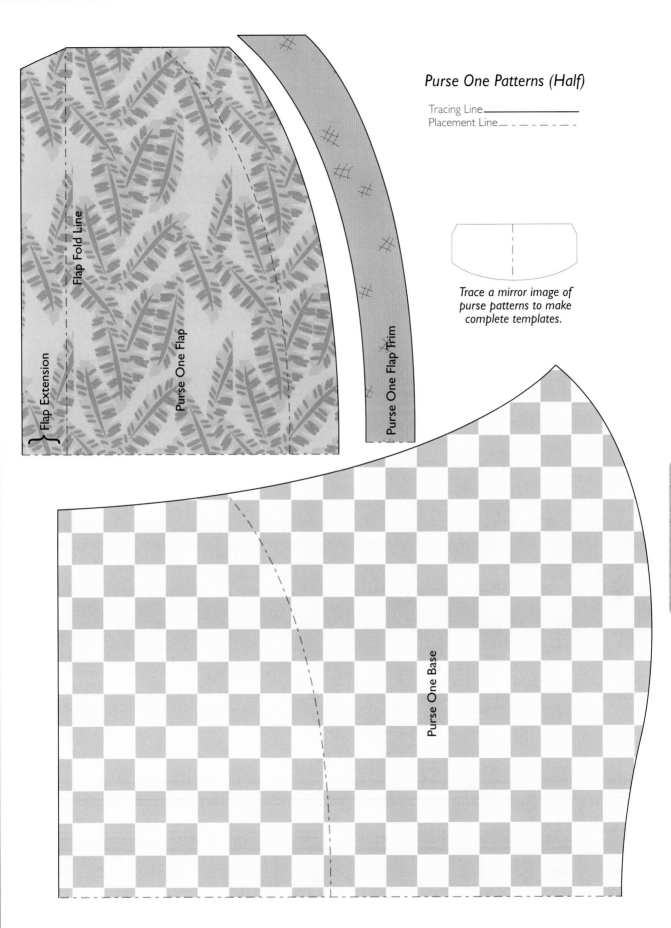

Purse One Patterns (Half)

Tracing Line ——————

Placement Line — · — · — · —

Flap Extension

Flap Fold Line

Purse One Flap

Purse One Flap Trim

Trace a mirror image of purse patterns to make complete templates.

Purse One Base

creative woman **STITCHES**

Handle

Purse Three Patterns (Half)

Tracing Line _____
Tracing Line _ _ _ _ _ _ _ _ _ _
(will be hidden behind other fabrics)
Placement Line _ . _ . _ . _ . _

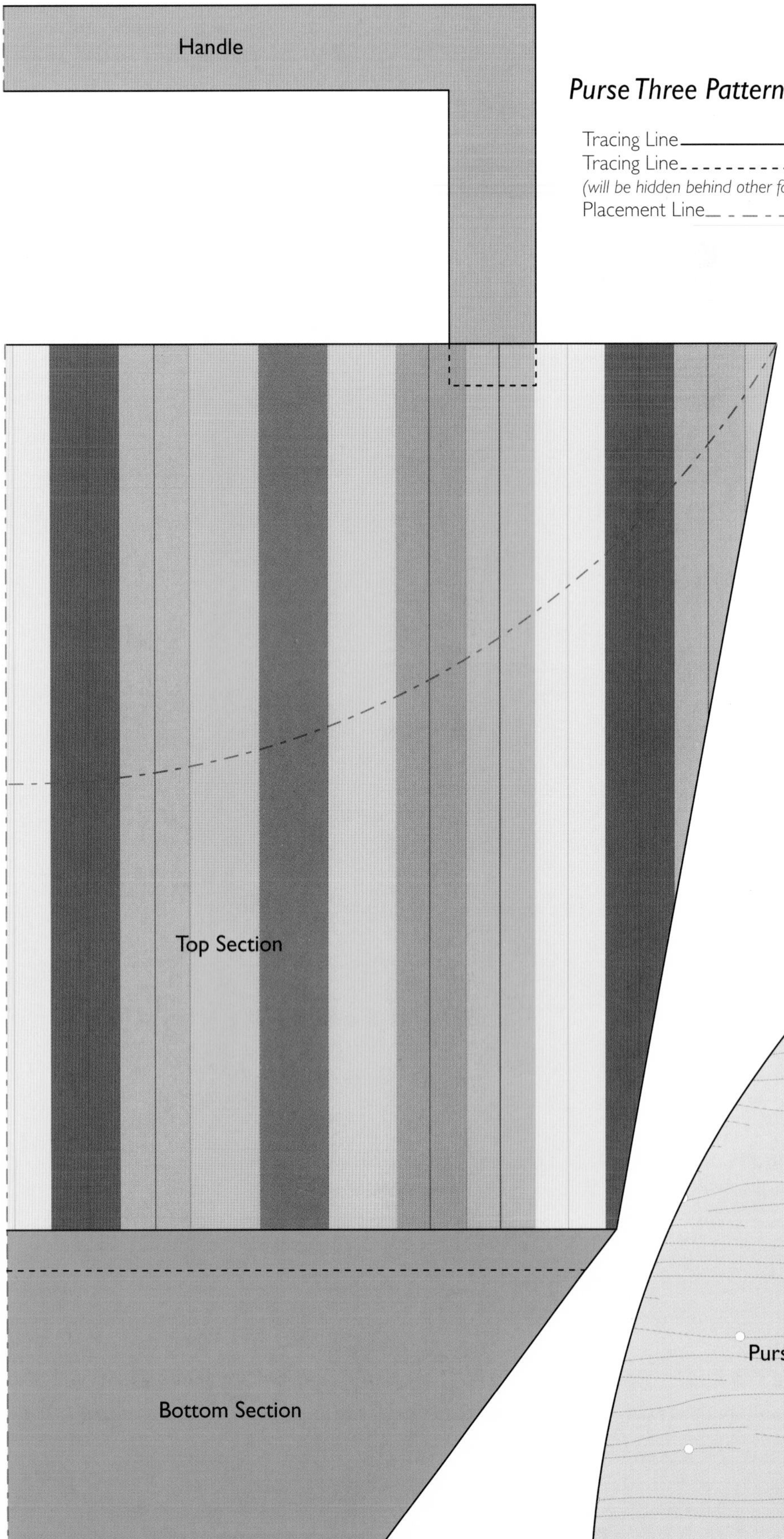

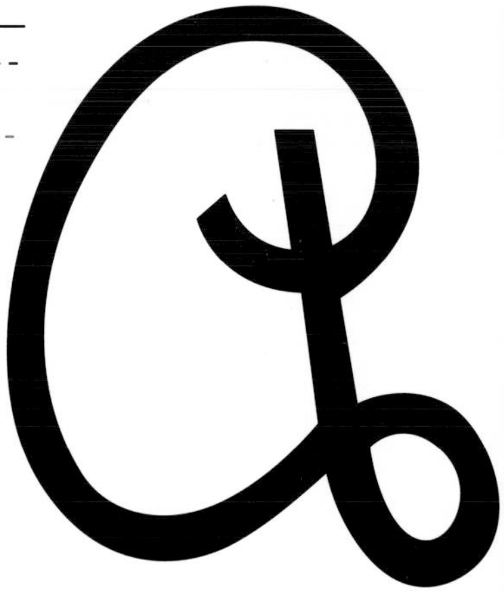

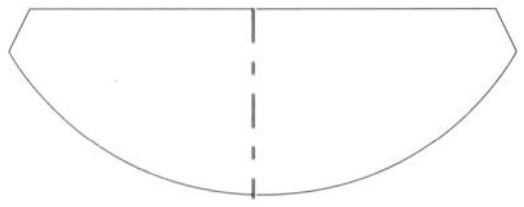

Trace a mirror image of purse patterns to make complete templates.

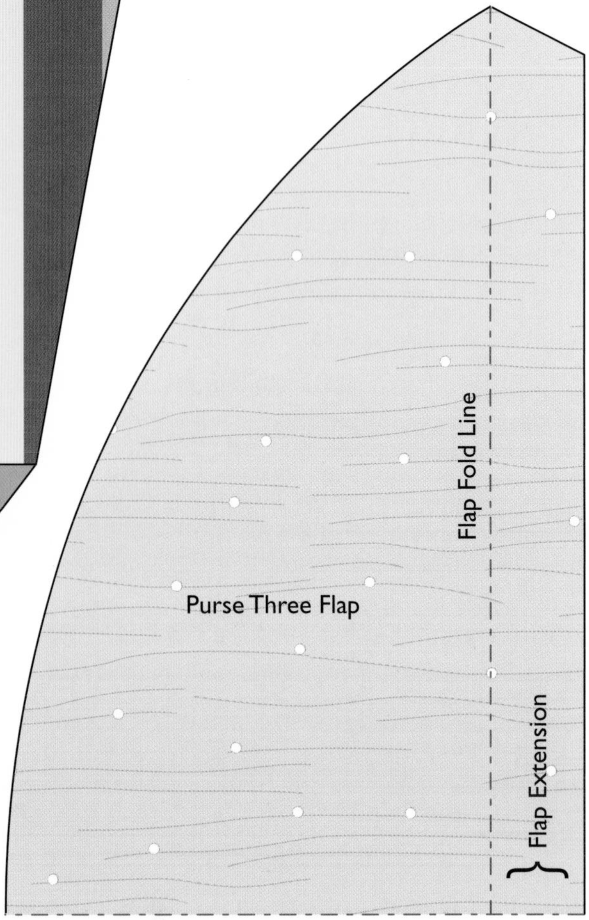

Top Section

Bottom Section

Purse Three Flap

Flap Fold Line

Flap Extension

The Creative Woman By Debbie Mumm®

Stitcher's Tote

Finished size: 15" high x 18" wide

Take your needlework with you wherever you go with this fun tote. Bright fabrics, whimsical trims, and hand embroidery make this tote a real stitcher's statement.

Materials Needed

Fabric A (Top) - ½ yard
  One 14" x 37" piece

Fabric B (Bottom) - ¼ yard
  One 6" x 37" piece
  Four 2" squares

Fabric C (Flap) - ¼ yard

Lining - ⅝ yard
  One 19" x 37" piece

Batting - 1⅛ yards
  One 21" x 39" piece
  One 7" x 20 piece

Backing - ⅝ yard
  One 21" x 39" piece

Decorative Trim - ⅔ yard

Perle Cotton

Purse Handles - 7"-wide

Plastic Canvas - 13" x 4"
(optional)

Assorted Buttons

Getting Started

Our tote is fully lined and embellished with decorative flap, hand embroidery, pompoms, buttons, and purchased handles. Please note that a combination of ½"-wide and ¼"-wide seams are used throughout.

Making the Tote Bag

1. Use Tote Bag Flap Pattern on page 67 to cut two Tote Bag Flap pieces from Fabric C.

2. Pin and baste decorative trim to curved edge of one flap piece as shown. (The pattern has ½"-wide seam allowance. Our trim was slightly narrower.)

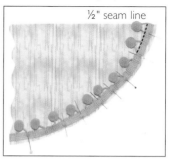

½" seam line

3. Place Tote Bag Flap pieces, right sides together, on 7" x 20" piece of batting. Stitch along curved edge using ½"-wide seam allowance. Trim batting close to stitching and even with straight edge. Trim seam to ¼" and clip tape of decorative trim, if needed. Turn flap right side out and press. Quilt as desired.

4. With right sides together and using a ½"-wide seam, sew 14" x 37" Fabric A to 6" x 37" Fabric B along one 37" side. Press seam open. Fold unit in half crosswise and mark center point of unit as shown.

Center Point

5. Layer 21" x 39" backing, 21" x 39" batting, and unit from step 4, referring to Layering the Quilt on page 110. Quilt as desired. Trim batting and backing even with Tote piece.

6. Referring to photo and Embroidery Stitch Guide on page 111, use perle cotton and a chevron stitch to embellish tote along seam line.

7. Pin flap to top of tote bag front between center point and ½" from side. Baste in place as shown.

Center Point

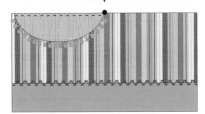

8. Fold Tote Bag unit, right sides together, in half crosswise and sew along side and bottom edges using ½"-wide seam. Press seam open.

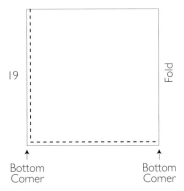

19

Fold

Bottom Corner   Bottom Corner

9. Fold bottom left corner of unit from step 8, matching side seam to bottom seam. Draw a 4" line across corner as shown. Sew on drawn line, anchoring stitches.

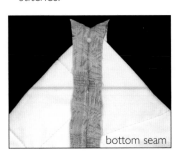

bottom seam

10. Repeat step 9 to fold bottom right corner of unit, matching fold to bottom seam. Draw a 4" line across corner and stitch on drawn line. Fold stitched corners to bottom seam of tote and tack in place for added stability.

bottom seam

Assembly

1. Fold 2" square Fabric B pieces in half, right sides together, and stitch using ¼"-wide seam allowance as shown. Turn right side out and press. Make four.

Fold

Make 4

2. Place units from step 1 through purse handle openings; center and pin to right side of flap as shown. Repeat matching placement on back of tote. Baste in place using a zipper foot.

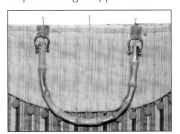

creative concepts

Fashion Frame
Finished size: 10" x 12"

Vintage patterns become artwork for the sewing room when you add a simple mat and frame.

Materials Needed for One Fashion Frame

Vintage Pattern Cover
9" x 11" Piece of Fabric
10" x 12" Purchased Frame (opening size is 7½" x 9½")
Double Stick Tape
Burnt Umber Glaze (Optional)
Matte Varnish

Making the Wall Art

1. *Remove pattern from envelope and trim envelope to fit inside frame, leaving ¾" of mat space on all sides.*

2. *Wrap fabric in a color that coordinates with pattern around the mat board that comes with the frame. Tape in place.*

3. *Mount pattern cover on fabric-covered mat board using double stick tape.*

4. *If desired, add an antique look to your frame. Remove glass from frame and apply burnt umber glaze, following the manufacturer's directions. Allow to dry. Spray frame with matte varnish.*

5. *Insert glass and mounted pattern cover into frame and hang as desired.*

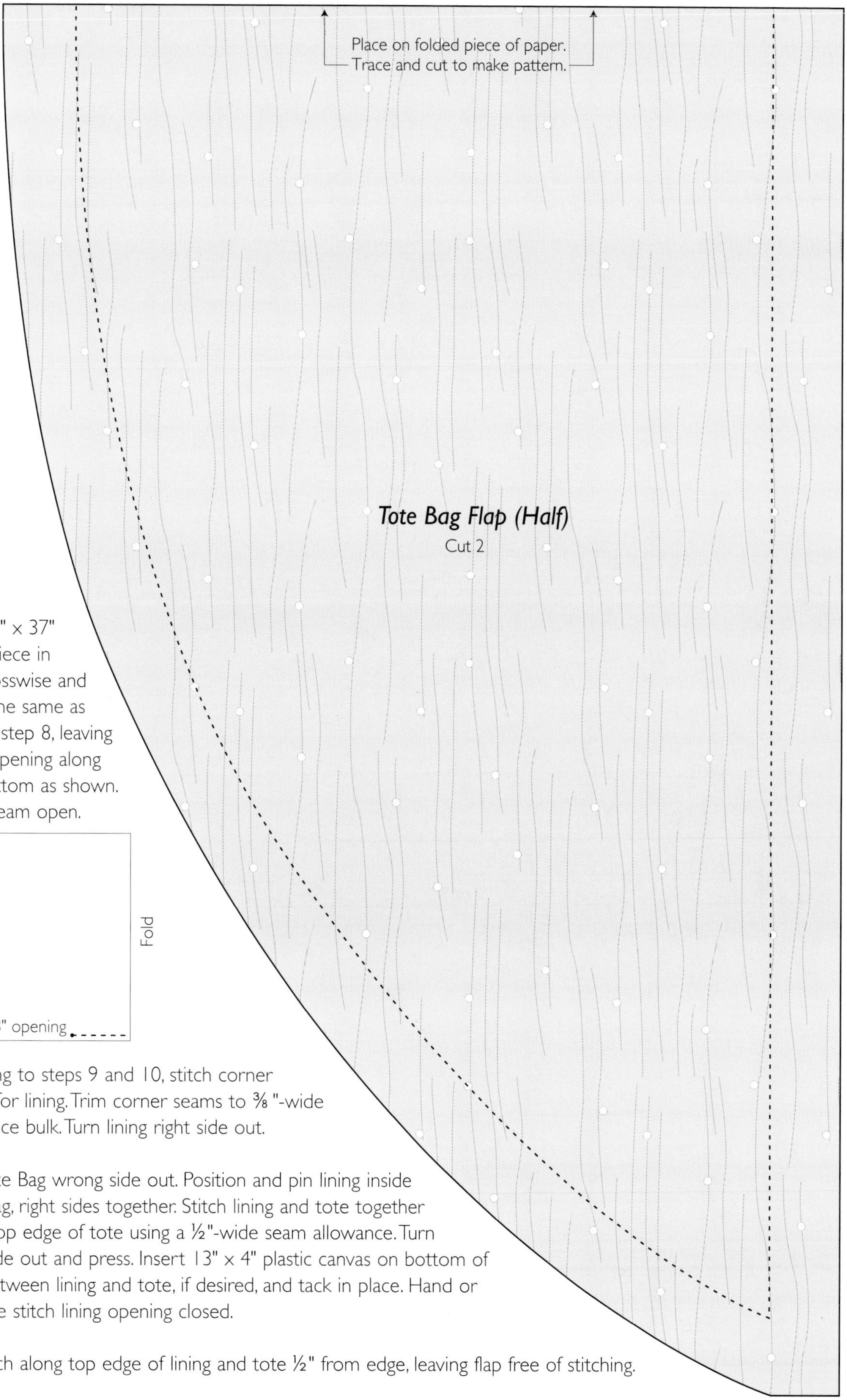

Place on folded piece of paper.
Trace and cut to make pattern.

Tote Bag Flap (Half)
Cut 2

3. Fold 19" × 37" lining piece in half crosswise and stitch the same as tote in step 8, leaving an 8" opening along the bottom as shown. Press seam open.

19

Fold

8" opening

4. Referring to steps 9 and 10, stitch corner seams for lining. Trim corner seams to ⅜"-wide to reduce bulk. Turn lining right side out.

5. Turn Tote Bag wrong side out. Position and pin lining inside Tote Bag, right sides together. Stitch lining and tote together along top edge of tote using a ½"-wide seam allowance. Turn right side out and press. Insert 13" × 4" plastic canvas on bottom of tote between lining and tote, if desired, and tack in place. Hand or machine stitch lining opening closed.

6. Top-stitch along top edge of lining and tote ½" from edge, leaving flap free of stitching.

7. Referring to photo, stack and sew buttons to flap.

The Creative Woman
Enjoys Nature

"I go to nature to be soothed and healed, and to have my senses put in order." ~John Burroughs

Hiking through the woods or strolling on a beach, Quilt Artist Karen Schoepflin Hagen finds inspiration and ideas everywhere for her quilts. "I try to get away from man-made activity," Karen states, "and out into the forest, the rural areas, the riverbanks, and beaches. I get so many ideas, I could make quilts for 300 years and not ever run out of ideas."

Karen Schoepflin Hagen

Karen makes sketches from memory, sometimes consulting references for accuracy. She chooses poses or angles that are artistically pleasing to her. Karen loves the fascinating array of prints and the endless textures and varieties of fabrics and feels free to use the fabric in new and interesting ways. For trees, Karen uses the frayed edges of fabric to softly blend the colors. "I'm always on the side of nature," Karen says. "Fabric naturally frays, why turn it under when it looks more natural in my compositions with frayed edges? I enjoy the limitations and the challenges of working with fabric."

Karen doesn't have any favorite colors and all combinations are exciting to her as long as they mimic nature. "Not all colors are beautiful in nature," Karen states. "You need dirt and dead grass!

Forest Floor Fragment by Karen Schoepflin Hagen

"Knowing trees, I understand the meaning of patience. Knowing grass, I can appreciate persistence." ~Hal Borland

Window to Nature Wall Quilt

| Window to Nature Wall Quilt 30" x 30" | FIRST CUT | |
	Number of Strips or Pieces	Dimensions
■ Fabric A *Green Scraps in assorted shades*	16 48	6½" squares 2½" squares
□ Fabric B *Gold Scraps in assorted shades*	6 16	6½" squares 2½" squares
□ Fabric C *Tan Scraps in assorted shades*	3	6½" squares

Backing - 1 yard
Batting - 34" x 34"
Tree Appliqué - ½ yard WoolFelt®
Leaf Appliqués - Assorted wool scraps
    for 38 large leaves and 8 small leaves
Temporary Fabric Adhesive Spray

Cutting Instructions

Read all instructions before beginning and use ¼"-wide seam allowances throughout. Read Cutting Strips and Pieces on page 108 prior to cutting fabrics.

Getting Started

This scrappy quilt includes twenty-five background blocks in a wide variety of green, gold, and tan fabrics. The blocks are made in five variations: four each of Blocks 1 and 3, twelve of Block 2, two each of Blocks 4 and 5, and one of Block 6. Blocks measure 6½" square unfinished.

The appliquéd tree is cut as one piece from Woolfelt™. It is not fused, but adhered to the quilt with temporary fabric adhesive, and stitched down with a straight stitch after the quilt is quilted.

Leaves are cut from a single layer of wool and added to the quilt in the final step. Refer to Accurate Seam Allowance on page 108. Whenever possible, use the Assembly Line Method on page 108. Press seams in direction of arrows.

Background Blocks

1. Refer to Quick Corner Triangles on page 108. Sew one 2½" Fabric A square to one contrasting 6½" Fabric A square as shown. Press. Make four in assorted fabric combinations and label Block 1.

Block 1

A = 2½ × 2½
A = 6½ × 6½
Make 4 in assorted fabrics

2. Making quick corner triangle units, sew two scrappy 2½" Fabric A squares to one contrasting 6½" Fabric A square. Make twelve in assorted fabric combinations and label Block 2. Press eight as shown, and four in opposite direction.

Block 2

A = 2½ × 2½
A = 6½ × 6½
Make 12 in assorted fabrics
(Press 8 as indicated and 4 in the opposite direction)

3. Making quick corner triangle units, sew three scrappy 2½" Fabric A squares and one 2½" Fabric B square to one contrasting 6½" Fabric B square as shown. Press. Make four in assorted fabric combinations and label Block 3.

Block 3

A = 2½ × 2½
B = 2½ × 2½
    6½ × 6½
Make 4 in assorted fabrics

4. Making quick corner triangle units, sew two scrappy 2½" Fabric A squares and two 2½" scrappy Fabric B squares to one contrasting 6½" Fabric B square as shown. Press. Make two in assorted fabric combinations. Label units Block 4. Repeat using two 2½"Fabric A squares, two 2½" Fabric B squares, and one 6½" Fabric C square as shown. Make two in assorted fabric combinations. Label units Block 5.

Block 4

A = 2½ × 2½
B = 2½ × 2½
    6½ × 6½
Make 2 in assorted fabrics

Block 5

A = 2½ × 2½
B = 2½ × 2½
C = 6½ × 6½
Make 2 in assorted fabrics

5. Making quick corner triangle units, sew four scrappy 2½" Fabric B squares to one 6½" Fabric C square as shown. Press. Label unit Block 6.

Block 6

B = 2½ × 2½
C = 6½ × 6½

Assembly

1. Sew two of Block 1 and three of Block 2 together as shown. Make two rows. Press one row as shown, and one in opposite direction.

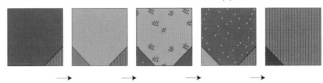

Make 2 (Rows 1 and 5)
(Press Row 5 in opposite direction)

2. Sew two of Block 2, two of Block 3, and one of Block 5 as shown. Press. Make two rows.

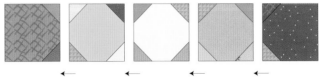

Make 2 (Rows 2 and 4)

3. Sew two of Block 2, two of Block 4, and Block 6 together, as shown, for Row 3. Press.

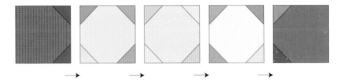

Window to Nature Wall Quilt
Finished size: 30" × 30"
Photo: page 68

4. Refer to layout on page 71 and photo. Arrange rows from steps 1-3 as shown. Sew rows together. Press.

Layering and Finishing

1. Layer top and backing right sides together over batting. Sew around perimeter of quilt top with ¼"-wide seam, leaving 10" opening for turning. Trim batting and backing, clip corners, turn right side out, and press. Hand-stitch opening closed.

2. Hand or machine quilt as desired.

3. Trace appliqué patterns on page 73-74 for tree, connecting trunk and limbs as shown to make a single tree unit. Trace large and small leaf patterns on page 77.

4. Cut one tree from WoolFelt™, and use assorted wool scraps to cut eight small leaves and thirty-eight large leaves.

5. Refer to layout on page 71 and photo. Use temporary spray adhesive to position tree in center of quilt as shown. Secure tree to quilt by sewing a straight stitch close to edge of appliqué.

6. Referring to layout on page 71 and photo, arrange and pin small leaves on tree branches as shown. Secure leaves in quilt with machine triple stitch or decorative stitching as desired, following stitching lines indicated on leaf pattern. Position and pin large leaves around perimeter of quilt as shown and secure in similar fashion.

The ever-changing lines, colors, and shapes of nature are an unfailing source of inspiration for any creative woman. Whether your real-life landscape is a city skyline or country lane, this wonderfully scrappy wall piece—with its sculptural, quick-stitched tree and richly colored, dimensional leaves— offers an inspirational window open all year long.

Lower Right Limb

Lower Left Limb

Tree Trunk

Window to Nature Patterns

Tracing Line ————————
Placement Line — · — · — · —

Window to Nature Patterns

Tracing Line ———————
Placement Line — — — —

Top Left Limb

Center Top Limbs

Trailing Leaves Vest

Celebrate your enjoyment of nature with this stylishly embellished vest.
Couched yarns and fibers and organza leaves add dramatic distinction to a fleece vest.

Materials Needed

Fleece Vest

Polyester Organza - ⅛ yard

Assorted Chenille Yarns and Fibers

Water Soluble Stabilizer

Five ⅜" Wooden Beads

Getting Started

Add outdoor charm to a purchased vest by using a simple couching technique to embellish with fiber accents and leaves. Check all materials' contents and care instructions to ensure they are compatible for cleaning. Extra lengths of fiber are left unstitched and beads are held in place with a knot, making removal easy for cleaning garment.

Embellishing the Vest

1. Referring to Window to Nature Leaf Patterns on page 77, trace five Small Leaves onto water soluble stabilizer. Place organza between two layers of stabilizer with marked piece on top.

2. Refer to Couching Technique on page 111 and photo. Place fiber on top of marked line and couch in place. Cut out leaf close to outside couched edge. Follow manufacturer's directions to remove stabilizer. Make five.

3. Referring to photo, arrange assorted fibers and leaves onto vest as desired. Mark placement lines with temporary fabric marker.

4. Referring to Couching Technique on page 111, couch fibers to vest, being careful not to stitch vest back or any pockets. Leave lower portions of fibers unstitched where leaves and beads will be attached.

5. Referring to embroidery line on Small Leaf Pattern (page 77), stitch leaves in place along center line.

6. String beads onto yarn or fibers and tie a knot to secure. Knot needs to be larger than center hole.

Dappled Leaves Planter

Leaves provide a pretty play of colors and texture on this handsome flowerpot planter. Leaf shapes are cut from sponge so this painting project is both easy and decorative.

Materials Needed

Terra Cotta Flowerpot

Gesso

Acrylic Craft Paints - Light, medium, medium/dark, and dark green; light and medium tan; medium and dark gold

Assorted Paintbrushes

Miracle Sponge™ *

Sea Sponge

Water-Based Burnt Umber Glaze

Matte Spray Varnish

Miracle Sponge™ is thinly compressed cellulose that expands when wet. It is available at many art and craft supply stores.

Painting the Planter

Note: Allow paint to dry thoroughly between applications.

1. Coat clean, dry, flowerpot with gesso, both inside and out, to prepare surface for painting. Allow to dry.

2. Base coat entire flowerpot with medium green paint. Be sure to paint at least 3" of the inside with the base color.

3. Place small amounts of medium green and medium/dark green paint on a palette or plastic plate. Dip sea sponge in water, wring thoroughly, then dip in both paints. Blot several times on paper towel to remove excess paint. Using a tapping motion, sponge color onto the medium green base coat, using a light touch for a stippled effect. Stipple entire exterior and at least 3" of interior. Allow to dry.

4. To prepare leaf-shaped sponges, transfer the patterns for the small and large leaves on page 77 onto paper. Tape the paper patterns to Miracle Sponge™ then use a craft knife or craft scissors to cut through paper and sponge. Dampen the Miracle Sponge™ leaves with water to make them expand. Wring thoroughly.

5. Leaves will be sponged onto flowerpot in layers starting with the largest and darkest leaves. Place a small amount of dark green paint on a palette or plastic plate. Using the large leaf-shaped sponge, rub into the dark green paint until sponge is covered. Blot on palette or paper towel.

   Carefully place leaf-shaped sponge on flowerpot and gently and evenly press sponge to transfer the paint onto the flowerpot. Repeat this process to randomly place large dark green leaves on flowerpot, leaving lots of space between leaves.

You should be able to apply two to three leaves before refilling sponge with paint. Rinse out sponge. Allow pot to dry.

6. Place a small amount of medium green and light green paint on palette or plastic plate. Rub large leaf-shaped sponge in both colors and, following the same techniques described in step 5, randomly sponge medium/light leaves onto flowerpot. Repeat, adding a few small leaves. These leaves will be more subtle and provide a background element. Rinse sponges and allow pot to dry.

7. Repeat process using a combination of medium and dark gold paint and the small leaf-shaped sponge. Place gold leaves so that they are random and some overlap the large leaves. Rinse sponge and allow pot to dry.

8. Repeat process using a combination of light and medium tan and the small leaf-shaped sponge. Rinse sponge and allow pot to dry.

9. Finish with some medium/ medium dark green leaves following the same process. Allow to dry.

10. Check flowerpot to make sure there is a good balance of colors. If there are empty spots or light or dark is needed in an area, sponge on a few more leaves.

11. When completely dry, apply burnt umber glaze following manufacturer's directions. This will make colors blend beautifully. If a darker color is desired, add additional coats of glaze. Allow to dry.

12. Spray flowerpot, inside and out, with matte varnish following manufacturer's directions.

Note: Do not plant directly into this flowerpot. Instead, plant in a smaller plastic flowerpot and place in painted flowerpot. Moisture from watering the plant can damage the painted surface.

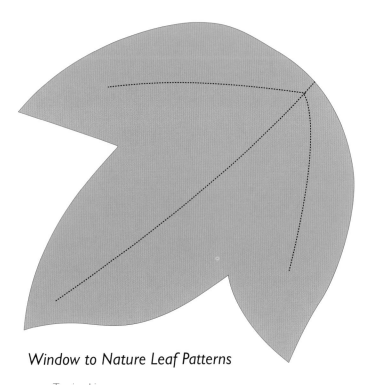

Window to Nature Leaf Patterns

Tracing Line————————
Embroidery Line............................

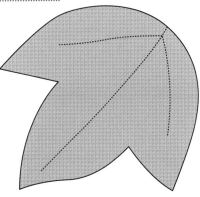

creative woman
ENJOYS NATURE

The Creative Woman
Decorates

"I have always loved decorating," declares Designer and Author Debbie Mumm. "I view a room as a large canvas just waiting for the layers of color and pattern to become something more than four walls. I believe that a well-appointed room is a creative means of self expression and an invitation to friends and family to enjoy the warmth I've created.

Other than paint, my favorite way to infuse a room with color and character is to use fabric. Fabric offers such a wide variety of colors, textures, and patterns...it is both a versatile and inspiring way to add ambiance to a home. From quilts to window coverings, table linens to pillows, fabric is such an easy and economical way to create soft furnishings in your home."

"The love of beauty, the service of it, the production of beautiful things, are the test and measure of the true worth of the individual and nation."

~From the Knight Errant 1892

Tips for Decorating with Fabric:
- Update a lampshade with fabric and trim.
- Accent pillows are a great way to make seasonal changes to a sofa.
- Chair cushions will add comfort and color to kitchen chairs.
- Quilted wallhangings and fabric art pieces are a great way to decorate the walls.
- Layers of luxurious pillows and bedding add elegance to a bedroom.

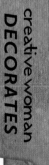

Blue Rhapsody Bed Quilt

Blue Rhapsody Bed Quilt 86" x 86"	FIRST CUT		SECOND CUT	
	Number of Strips or Pieces	Dimensions	Number of Pieces	Dimensions
Directional fabric is not recommended for backgrounds.				
Fabric A *Dark Background* *1½ yards*	3 2 2	9½" x 42" 8" x 42" 2" x 42"	4 8 8 24	9½" squares 9½" x 8" 8" squares 2" squares
Fabric B *Light Background* *1⅛ yards*	2 2 1	9½" x 42" 8" x 42" 2" x 42"	8 8 16	9½" x 8" 8" squares 2" squares
Fabric C *Dark Diagonal Accent* *1⅙ yards*	6	6½" x 42"	36	6½" squares
Fabric D *Light Diagonal Accent* *¾ yard*	5	4½" x 42"	36	4½" squares
Fabric E *Medium Diagonal Accent* *½ yard*	4	3½" x 42"	36	3½" squares
Fabric F *Center Squares* *5/8yard*	5	3⅜" x 42"	52	3⅜" squares
Fabric G *Dark Sashing* *1 yard**	3	11" x 42"	60	11" x 2"*
Fabric H *Light Sashing* *1 yard*	16	2" x 42"	20 40 48	2" x 9½" 2" x 8" 2" squares
BORDERS				
First Border *⅜ yard*	7	1½" x 42"		
Second Border *½ yard*	7	2" x 42"		
Third Border *7/8yard*	8	3½" x 42"		
Outside Border *1½ yards*	8	6" x 42"		
Binding *¾ yard*	9	2¾" x 42"		

Backing - 7⅞yards
Batting - 94" x 94"
**For directional fabric, the measurement that is listed first runs parallel to selvage (strip width).*

Cutting Instructions

Read all instructions before beginning and use ¼"-wide seam allowances throughout. Read Cutting Strips and Pieces on page 108 prior to cutting fabrics.

Getting Started

This quilt includes nine blocks in three variations: four Corner Blocks, four Side Blocks, and one Center Block. The blocks are constructed from various combinations of seven different units. When set side-by-side, the blocks create a strong overall design. Blocks measure 21½" square unfinished.

Directional fabric is not recommended for Fabric A and B pieces. If you choose to use a directional fabric, adjust yardage and check placement of individual pieces prior to sewing. Refer to Accurate Seam Allowance on page 108. Whenever possible, use the Assembly Line Method on page 108. Press seams in direction of arrows.

Making the Blocks

1. Refer to Quick Corner Triangles on page 108. Sew one 2" Fabric A square to one 11" x 2" Fabric G piece as shown. Press. Make eight A/G units. Sew one 2" Fabric B square to one 11" x 2" Fabric G piece. Press. Make four B/G units.

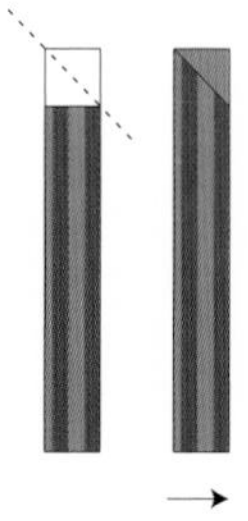

A = 2 x 2
G = 11 x 2
Make 8 A/G units

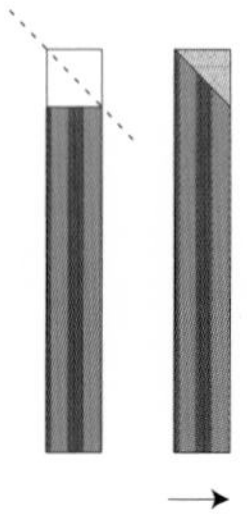

B = 2 x 2
G = 11 x 2
Make 4 B/G units

2. Making a quick corner triangle unit, sew one 2" Fabric H square to one 11" × 2" Fabric G piece as shown. Press. Make forty-eight H/G units.

H = 2 × 2
G = 11 × 2
Make 48 H/G units

3. Making a quick corner triangle unit, sew one 2" Fabric A square to one H/G unit from step 2 as shown. Press. Make four A/H/G units. Sew one 2" Fabric B square to one H/G unit as shown. Press. Make four B/H/G units.

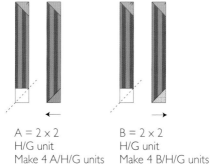

A = 2 × 2
H/G unit
Make 4 A/H/G units

B = 2 × 2
H/G unit
Make 4 B/H/G units

4. Making a quick corner triangle unit, sew one 2" Fabric A square to one 2" × 9½" Fabric H piece as shown. Press. Make twelve A/H units, four of one variation and eight of the other variation.

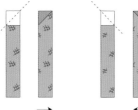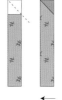

A = 2 × 2
H = 2 × 9½
Make 8 A/H units

A = 2 × 2
H = 2 × 9½
Make 4 A/H units

5. Making a quick corner triangle unit, sew one 2" Fabric B square to one 2" × 9½" Fabric H piece as shown. Press. Make eight B/H units, four of each variation.

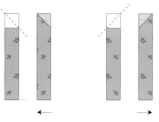

B = 2 × 2
H = 2 × 9½
Make 8 B/H units
(4 of each variation)

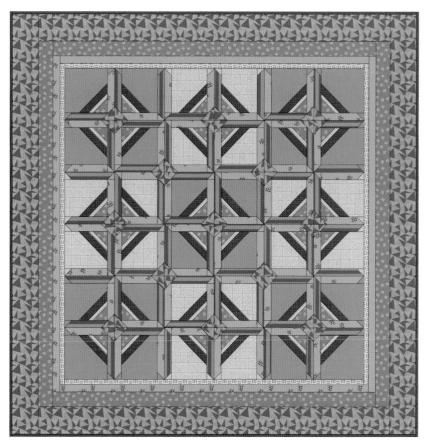

Blue Rhapsody Bed Quilt
Finished size: 86" × 86"
Photo: page 78

6. Making a quick corner triangle unit, sew one 4½" Fabric D square to one 6½" Fabric C square as shown. Press. Make thirty-six.

D = 4½ × 4½
C = 6½ × 6½
Make 36

7. Making a quick corner triangle unit, sew one 3½" Fabric E square to one unit from step 6 as shown. Press. Make thirty-six.

E = 3½ × 3½
Unit from Step 6
Make 36

8. Making a quick corner triangle unit, sew one unit from step 7 to one 9½" Fabric A square as shown. Prior to stitching, flip back unit to see if positioning is correct. Press. Make four.

Unit from Step 7
A = 9½ × 9½
Make 4

creative concepts

Rhapsody Pillow
Finished size: 14" square

You'll hit just the right note with a harmonious pillow to complement your Blue Rhapsody Quilt.

Materials Needed

Center - Scrap
  One 4½" square
First Border - ⅛ yard
  Two 1½" x 6½" pieces
  Two 1½" x 4½" pieces
Second Border - ⅛ yard
  Two 1½" x 8½" pieces
  Two 1½" x 6½" pieces
Third Border - ⅛ yard
  Two 1" x 9½" pieces
  Two 1" x 8½" pieces
Fourth Border - ⅛ yard
  Two 1" x 10½" pieces
  Two 1" x 9½" pieces
Outside Border and Backing - ½ yard
  Two 10" x 14½" strips
  Two 2½" x 14½" strips
  Two 2½" x 10½" strips
Lining - ½ yard
  One 17" square
Batting - One 17" square
14" Pillow Form

Making the Pillow

1. Refer to diagrams on page 89 for steps 1 and 2. Sew 4½" Center square between two 1½" x 4½" First Border pieces. Press seams toward First Border. Sew two 1½" x 6½" First Border pieces to remaining sides. Press seams toward each newly added border throughout.

2. Sew unit from step 1 between two 1½" x 6½" Second Border pieces. Press. Sew two 1½" x 8½" Second Border pieces to remaining sides. Press.

3. Sew unit from step 2 between two 1" x 8½" Third Border pieces. Press. Sew two 1" x 9½" Third Border pieces to remaining sides. Press.

4. Sew unit from step 3 between two 1" x 9½" Fourth Border pieces. Press. Sew two 1" x 10½" Fourth Border pieces to remaining sides. Press.

5. Sew unit from step 4 between two 2½" x 10½" Outside Border strips.

Press. Sew two 2½" x 14½" Outside Border strips to remaining sides. Pres

6. Refer to Finishing Pillows step 1, page 111, to quilt pillow. Refer to steps 2-4 to sew 10" x 14½" Backing pieces to pillow. Refer to Pillow Forms page 111, to make pillow form, if desired.

9. Sew one unit from step 8 to one A/H unit from step 4 as shown. Press. Make four. Sew this unit to one A/G unit from step 1 as shown. Press. Make four.

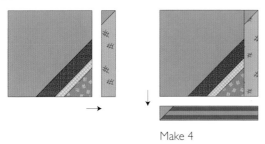

Make 4

10. Making a quick corner triangle unit, sew one 3⅜ " Fabric F square to one unit from step 9 as shown. Press. Make four. Label these Unit 1. Unit 1 measures 11" square.

Unit 1

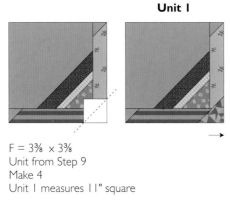

F = 3⅜ × 3⅜
Unit from Step 9
Make 4
Unit 1 measures 11" square

11. Making a quick corner triangle unit, sew one unit from step 7 to one 9½" × 8" Fabric A piece as shown. Prior to stitching, flip back unit to see if positioning is correct. Press. Make eight, four of each variation.

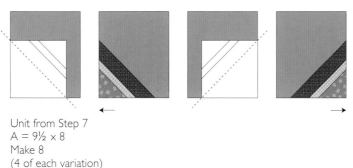

Unit from Step 7
A = 9½ × 8
Make 8
(4 of each variation)

12. Making a quick corner triangle unit, sew one unit from step 7 to one 9½" × 8" Fabric B piece as shown. Prior to stitching, flip back unit to see if positioning is correct. Press. Make eight, four of each variation.

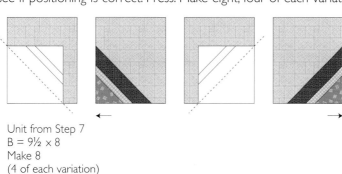

Unit from Step 7
B = 9½ × 8
Make 8
(4 of each variation)

13. Sew one unit from step 11 to one 2" × 8" Fabric H piece as shown. Press. Make four. Sew one unit from step 12 to one 2" × 8" Fabric H piece as shown. Press. Make four.

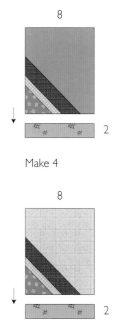

8

2

Make 4

8

2

Make 4

14. Sew one unit from step 13 between one A/G unit from step 1 and one A/H/G unit from step 3 as shown. Press. Make four. Sew one unit from step 13 between one B/G unit from step 1 and one B/H/G unit from step 3 as shown. Press. Make four.

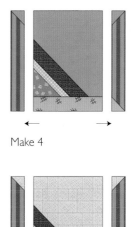

Make 4

Make 4

creative woman
DECORATES

15. Making a quick corner triangle unit, sew one 3⅜" Fabric F square to one unit from step 14 as shown. Press. Make eight, four of each combination. Label these Unit 2 and Unit 3. Units measure 11" square.

Unit 2

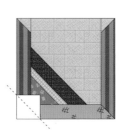

Unit 3

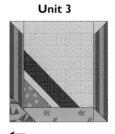

F = 3⅜ × 3⅜
Unit from Step 14
Make 8
(4 of each combination)
Units 2 and 3 measure 11" square

16. Sew one unit from step 11 between one of each A/H variation from step 4 as shown. Press. Make four. Sew one unit from step 12 between one of each B/H variation from step 5 as shown. Press. Make four. Sew each unit to one H/G unit from step 2 as shown. Press. Make eight, four of each combination.

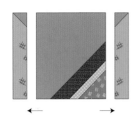 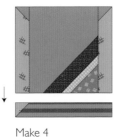

Make 4

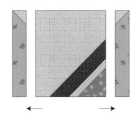 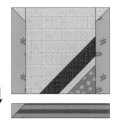

Make 4

17. Making a quick corner triangle unit, sew one 3⅜" Fabric F square to one of each unit from step 16 as shown. Press. Make eight, four of each combination. Label these Unit 4 and Unit 5. Units measure 11" square.

Unit 4

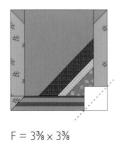 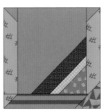

Unit 5

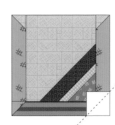 

F = 3⅜ × 3⅜
Units from Step 16
Make 8
(4 of each combination)
Units 4 and 5 measure 11" square

18. Making a quick corner triangle unit, sew one unit from step 7 to one 8" Fabric A square as shown. Prior to stitching, flip back unit to see if positioning is correct. Press. Make eight. Sew one unit from step 7 to one 8" Fabric B square as shown. Press. Make eight.

Unit from Step 7
A = 8" × 8"
Make 8

Unit from Step 7
B = 8" × 8"
Make 8

19. Sew one unit from step 18 between two 2" × 8" Fabric H pieces as shown. Press. Make sixteen, eight of each combination.

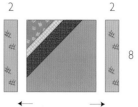

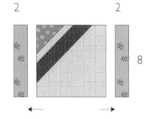

Make 16
(8 of each combination)

20. Sew each unit from step 19 between two H/G units from step 2 as shown. Press. Make sixteen, eight of each combination.

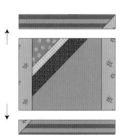

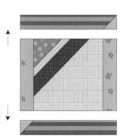

Make 16
(8 of each combination)

If you like your jazz "cool" and your décor sleek and contemporary, you'll love the up-to-the-minute good looks of this striking bed quilt. The pattern is clean and linear, the palette crisp and airy…and you'll be pleased to know that our time-saving techniques are as cutting edge as the quilt's design.

creative woman
DECORATES

21. Making quick corner triangle units, sew two 3⅜ " Fabric F squares to each unit from step 20 as shown. Press. Make sixteen, eight of each combination. Label these Unit 6 and Unit 7. Units measure 11" square.

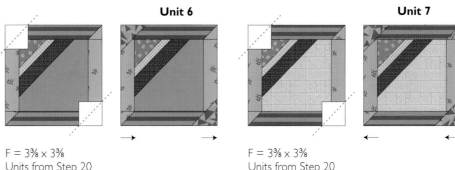

Unit 6

F = 3⅜ x 3⅜
Units from Step 20
Make 8
Unit 6 measures 11" square

Unit 7

F = 3⅜ x 3⅜
Units from Step 20
Make 8
Unit 7 measures 11" square

22. Arrange Unit 1, Unit 2, Unit 4 and Unit 6 as shown. Sew units into rows. Press. Sew rows together. Press. Make four blocks. Label these Corner Block. Blocks measure 21½" square.

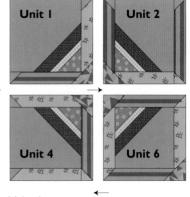

Make 4
Corner Blocks measure 21½" square

23. Arrange Unit 5, Unit 3, and two Unit 7s as shown. Sew units into rows. Press. Sew rows together. Press. Make four blocks. Label these Side Block. Blocks measure 21½" square.

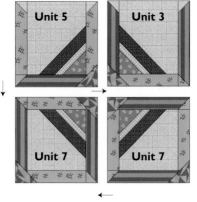

Make 4
Side Blocks measure 21½" square

24. Arrange and sew four of Unit 6 as shown. Press. Sew units into rows. Press. Sew rows together. Press. Label this Center Block. Block measures 21½" square.

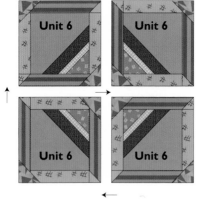

Re-press as needed
Center Block measures 21½" square

Assembly

1. Refer to photo on page 85 and layout on page 81. Arrange and sew blocks in three horizontal rows of three blocks each noting direction of blocks. Press seams in opposite directions from row to row.

2. Sew rows together. Press.

Borders

1. Sew 1½" x 42" First Border strips end-to-end to make one continuous 1½"-wide strip. Press. Refer to Adding the Borders on page 110. Measure quilt through center from side to side. Cut two 1½"-wide First Border strips to that measurement. Sew to top and bottom of quilt. Press seams toward border.

2. Measure quilt through center from top to bottom, including borders just added. Cut two 1½"-wide First Border strips to that measurement. Sew to sides of quilt. Press.

3. Refer to steps 1 and 2 to join, measure, trim, and sew 2"-wide Second Border strips, 3½"-wide Third Border strips, and 6"-wide Outside Border strips to top, bottom, and sides of quilt. Press seams toward last border added.

Layering and Finishing

1. Cut backing crosswise into three equal pieces. Sew pieces together to make one 94" x 120" (approximate) backing piece. Press and trim to 94" x 94".

2. Arrange and baste backing, batting, and top together, referring to Layering the Quilt on page 110.

3. Hand or machine quilt as desired.

4. Sew 2¾" x 42" binding strips end-to-end to make one continuous 2¾"-wide strip. Refer to Binding the Quilt on page 110 and bind quilt to finish.

creative concepts

Rhapsody Pillow Coverings

Finished sizes: 21" x 55" and 21" x 27"

Add pizzazz to your bed with this inspired pillow treatment. One large pillow adds sleek comfort and two covers dress your standard bed pillows during daylight hours.

Materials Needed

Pillows - One 20" x 54" and
 Two 20" x 26"
Body Pillow Cover - 2⅞ yards
 One 21½" x 55½" piece (Front)
 Two 21½" x 30½" pieces (Backing)
Standard Pillow Covers - 2½ yards
 Two 21½" x 27½" pieces (Front)
 Four 21½" x 16½" pieces (Backing)

To adjust fabric quantity for different size pillows, measure width and length of pillow. For pillow front fabric, add 1½" to width and length measurements. Cut one piece of fabric by this measurement for pillow front.

For pillow backing fabric, the width will be the same as the front width. The length of the pillow backing fabric, will be half the length of pillow front fabric measurement plus 2¾". Cut two pieces of fabric by these measurements for the backing.

For example:
27" width x 60" length pillow

Pillow Front: (cut 1)
 27" + 1½" = 28½" width
 60" + 1½" = 61½" length
Pillow Back: (cut 2)
 28½" width
 61½" divided by two = 30¾"
 30¾" + 2¾" = 33½" length

Making the Pillow Coverings

Refer to Finishing Pillows page 110, steps 2-4 to sew backing pieces to pillow front.

Rhapsody Head Board

Finished size: 17" x 60" (each panel)

Make a dramatic decorating statement with this stylish complement to our beautiful Blue Rhapsody Bed Quilt (page 78). The quilted and wood-based panels feature dynamic dimensional accents, including a separately mounted and attached block, layered hand appliqué, and a neatly piped border.

Cutting Instructions

Read all instructions before beginning and use ¼"-wide seam allowances throughout. Read Cutting Strips and Pieces on page 108 prior to cutting fabrics.

Getting Started

This project includes three separate fabric panels. Fabric panels measure 23½" x 66" before attaching to boards. Each panel is assembled and quilted, then stretched and stapled to a 17" x 60" piece of wood. A hand-appliquéd accent strip is attached to each quilted panel; this prevents any distortion of the strips due to the stretching process.

The center panel features a pieced block that is quilted, stretched, and stapled separately to a 9" wood square, then attached to the center panel with screws. Side panels are accented with a piped border unit. Whenever possible, use the Assembly Line Method on page 108. Press seams in direction of arrows.

Rhapsody Headboard 17" x 60" each panel	FIRST CUT	
	Number of Strips or Pieces	Dimensions
Fabric A *Background* 3¾ yards	1	66" x 23½"
	2	66" x 13½"
Fabric B *Light Appliqué Stripe* ⅜ yard	1	3½" x 23½"
	2	3½" x 11½"
	1	2" x 23½"
	2	2" x 11½"
Fabric C *Dark Appliqué Stripe* ⅙ yard	1	2" x 23½"
	2	2" x 11½"
Fabric D *Center Square* Scrap	1	4½" square
Fabric E *1st Accent* ⅛ yard	2	1½" x 6½"
	2	1½" x 4½"
Fabric F *2nd Accent & Piping* ½ yard	4	3" x 42"
	2	1½" x 8½"
	2	1½" x 6½"

Rhapsody Headboard continued	FIRST CUT	
	Number of Strips or Pieces	Dimensions
Fabric G *Outside Accent* ¼ yard	2	3" x 13½"
	2	3" x 8½"
First Border ¼ yard	4	1½" x 42"
Second Border ⅓ yard	4	2½" x 42"
Outside Border 1 yard	4	7½" x 42"

Backing (does not show) - 6 yards
 Three 27" x 70" and one 15" square
Batting - Three 27" x 70" & one 15" square
⅜ " Cording - 3¾ yards
½" Particle Board or Plywood -
 Three 17" x 60" pieces and
 one 9" square piece
¾" Wood Screws, Hanging Brackets,
 Staple Gun & Staples

The Creative Woman By Debbie Mumm®

Accent Block

1. Sew one 4½" Fabric D square between two 1½" × 4½" Fabric E pieces. Press. Sew this unit between two 1½" × 6½" Fabric E pieces as shown. Press.

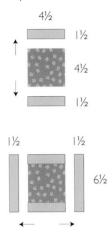

2. Sew unit from step 1 between two 1½" × 6½" Fabric F pieces as shown. Press. Sew this unit between two 1½" × 8½" Fabric F pieces. Press.

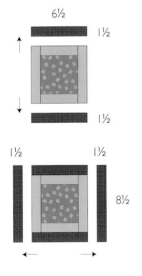

3. Sew unit from step 2 between two 3" × 8½" Fabric G pieces as shown. Press. Sew this unit between two 3" × 13½" Fabric G pieces. Press. Block measures 13½" square.

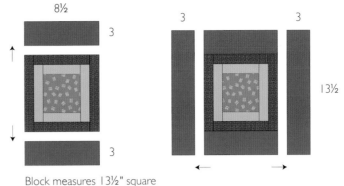

Block measures 13½" square

4. Arrange and baste 15" backing square, 15" batting square, and block together, referring to Layering the Quilt on page 110. Hand or machine quilt as desired.

Rhapsody Head Board
Finished size: 17" × 60" (each panel)
Photo: page 88

creative woman
DECORATES

5. Center quilted block face up over 9" wood square. Pull sides of block snugly over edges of wood, checking that equal amounts of Outside Border are visible on all sides. Use staple gun to secure all sides of quilted square to wood. Staple from center, working toward corners, stretching and checking Outside Border placement. Come close to, but do not staple, corners. Trim excess batting from corners, making sure to leave batting along side edges.

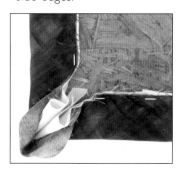

6. Pull fabric tightly at corner and staple. Trim excess fabric as shown.

7. Pull one side of corner tightly and staple as shown.

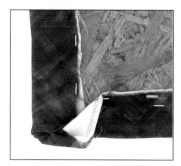

8. Pull remaining side of corner tightly and staple as shown.

9. Repeat steps 6-8 to finish remaining corners.

Center Panel

1. Arrange and baste 27" x 70" backing piece, 27" x 70" batting piece, and 66" x 23½" Fabric A piece together, referring to Layering the Quilt on page 110. Hand or machine quilt as desired. Trim backing and batting even with Fabric A.

2. Refer to Accent Block, steps 5-9 to attach quilted panel to 17" x 60" wood piece.

3. Sew 2" x 23½" Fabric B strip and 2" x 23½" Fabric C strip together to make a strip set. Press seams toward Fabric C.

4. Layer strip set from step 2 and 3½" x 23½" Fabric B strip right sides together. Using ¼" -wide seam, stitch along both 23½" sides, leaving short ends open for turning. Turn right side out and press.

5. Refer to photo on page 88 and layout on page 89. Position unit from step 4 on quilted panel 7" from top edge as shown. Refer to Hand Appliqué on page 109 to pin and stitch unit in place. Wrap edges to back and stitch in place.

6. Referring to photo on page 88 and layout on page 89, center Accent Block on appliqué section of panel as shown. Use screws to attach block to panel from back.

Side Panels

1. Sew 3" x 42" Fabric F strips end-to-end to make one continuous 3"-wide strip. Press. Wrap cording with fabric strip (wrong sides together) and use a zipper or cording foot to machine baste close to cording to make piping. Trim ¼" away from stitches. Cut into two 66"-long strips.

2. Place 13½" × 66" Fabric A strip, right sides together with piping strip. Baste, sewing from wrong side of Fabric A. Make two.

3. Sew 1½" × 42" First Border strips end-to-end to make one continuous 1½"-wide strip. Repeat with 2½"-wide Second Border strips and 7½"-wide Outside Border strips.

4. Sew First, Second, and Outside Border strips from step 3 together, as shown, staggering seams. Press. Cut into two 66"-long Border units.

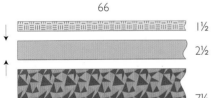

5. With right sides together, sew border unit from step 4 to unit from step 2. Press. Make two.

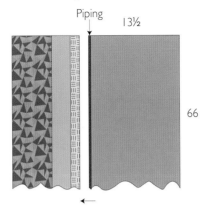

Make 2

6. Arrange and baste 27" × 70" backing piece, 27" × 70" batting piece, and unit from step 5 together, referring to Layering the Quilt on page 110. Make two. Hand or machine quilt as desired. Trim backing and batting even with pieced unit.

7. Refer to Accent Block, steps 5-9, to attach quilted panel to 17" × 60" wood piece. Make two.

8. Sew one 2" × 11½" Fabric B strip and one 2" × 11½" Fabric C strip together lengthwise to make a strip set. Press seams toward Fabric C. Make two.

9. Mark midpoint of one short side of 3½" × 11½" Fabric B piece as shown. Measure and mark top and bottom edge 1¾" from corners. Using marks for guidance, trim two corners from Fabric B piece as shown. Make two.

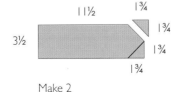

Make 2

10. Layer unit from step 8 and trimmed Fabric B piece from step 9 right sides together. Using ¼" seam, stitch around edges of Fabric B piece as shown, leaving short end open for turning. Clip corners, turn right side out, and press. Make two, one of each variation.

Make 2
(1 of each variation)

11. Refer to photo on page 88 and layout on page 89. Position unit from step 10 on quilted panels 7" from top edge as shown. Refer to Hand Appliqué on page 109 to pin and stitch unit in place. Wrap unfinished edge to back and stitch in place. Make two.

Finishing

Attach hanging brackets to back of each panel. Referring to photo on page 88, hang panels on wall behind bed, spacing panels 3" apart or as desired.

< Gardening
and quilting
go hand in hand for
quilter and
master gardener,
Sue Bates.

TIPS
For Garden-Inspired Quilts:

~ Take photos of particularly pleasing areas in the garden. Use the photos as color references and inspiration for watercolor quilts.

~ While you have the camera out, take close-ups of favorite flowers to use for appliqués and possible quilting templates.

~ In winter, consult seed catalogs and wildflower books for garden inspiration.

"My garden is a constant inspiration for my quilts," says Master Gardener Sue Bates. "Gardening and nature give me the know-how to combine colors in a pleasing way. Looking at the garden helps me to understand the many different shades of a single color, like green, for example. Every plant is a different color of green and the hues change throughout the day depending on the light. I especially love early morning when dew adds a glow to the garden. I use my observation of colors in the garden to help me select just the right hues in a pleasing combination for all of my quilts."

"I also look to the garden for inspiration for quilt designs," Sue adds. "If I'm intrigued by a certain flower, it will soon show up in both my garden and my quilts!"

Quilter and Gardener
Maureen Cramer >
looks at gardening and quilting
in a different way...

"There are only two things in the world over which I have the utmost control," Maureen says. "With both gardening and quilting, I have the freedom to create my own beautiful world."

"If something doesn't look right in the garden, I can ungarden, just as I can unsew in my quilting projects," Maureen quips. "In the garden, I'm working with nature rather than fabric and thread, but I am the designer, and I get to decide what goes where."

The Creative Woman
Gardens

To plant a garden is to believe in tomorrow.
To sew a quilt is to believe in today.

Favorite Flowers Lap Quilt

Favorite Flowers Lap Quilt 47½" x 58½"	FIRST CUT	
	Number of Strips or Pieces	Dimensions
GARDEN LILY BLOCK		
Background ⅜ yard	1	12½" x 23½"
First Border ⅛ yard	2 2	1½" x 25½" 1½" x 12½"
Second Border ¼ yard	2 2	2½" x 29½" 2½" x 14½"
SNAIL BLOCK		
Background ¼ yard	1	7½" x 16½"
Border ⅛ yard	2 2	1½" x 16½" 1½" x 9½"
VINE BLOCK		
Background ⅝ yard*	1	20½" x 4½"

For directional fabric, the measurement that is listed first runs parallel to selvage (strip width).

GERANIUM BLOCK		
Background ⅜ yard	1	10½" x 16½"
First Border ⅛ yard	2 2	1" x 17½" 1" x 10½"
Second Border ⅙ yard	2 2	2" x 20½" 2" x 11½"

Favorite Flowers Lap Quilt continued	FIRST CUT	
	Number of Strips or Pieces	Dimensions
POTTED DAISIES BLOCK		
Background ⅜ yard	1 2 2 2	10½" x 23½" 2½" x 3½" 2½" squares 1½" squares
Pot Rim ⅛ yard	1	1½" x 21½"
Pot Accent ⅛ yard	1	1½" x 19½"
Flowerpot ⅛ yard	1	2½" x 19½"
First Border ⅛ yard	2 2	1½" x 23½" 1½" x 16½"
Second Border ¼ yard	2 2	1½" x 25½" 1½" x 18½"
DAISY BLOCK		
Background Scrap	1	9½" square
VIOLA BLOCK		
Background Scrap	1	9½" square
Accent Corners ¼ yard	4	5" squares

Favorite Flowers Lap Quilt continued	FIRST CUT	
	Number of Strips or Pieces	Dimensions
BORDERS		
Quilt First Border ⅓ yard	5	2" x 42"
Quilt Second Border ¼ yard	5	1¼" x 42"
Outside Border ⅝ yard	5	3½" x 42"
Binding ⅝ yard	6	2¾" x 42"

Backing - 3 yards
Batting - 54" x 65"
Flower, Leaf, Stem, and Snail Appliqués - Assorted scraps
Cording - 1 yard red, 1 yard green, ⅜ yard dark green
Seven Assorted Black Buttons
Assorted Beads - 21 small black beads; 9 red beads; 3 yellow beads
Embroidery Floss - Green, tan, and black
Lightweight Fusible Web - 1½ yards
Heavyweight Fusible Web - ⅛ yard

Cutting Instructions

Read all instructions before beginning and use ¼"-wide seam allowances throughout. Read Cutting Strips and Pieces on page 108 prior to cutting fabrics.

Getting Started

This quilt includes seven blocks in varying sizes, each featuring a different floral motif. Some of the blocks include piecing and embellishment, some are framed with borders, and all include quick-fuse appliqué. Refer to Accurate Seam Allowance on page108. Press seams in direction of arrows. To keep construction simple, you'll find yardages, block layouts, and specific step-by-step instructions listed separately for each block. Information common to all blocks appears in Making the Blocks.

Making the Blocks

Refer to appliqué instructions on page 109. Our instructions are for Quick-Fuse Appliqué. Unless instructed otherwise, use lightweight fusible web for all appliqués. If you prefer hand appliqué, reverse templates and add ¼"-wide seam allowances. Refer to individual patterns, pages 98, 100, 101, 102, and 105 for number of regular and reversed appliqué pieces needed for each block. Photo on page 92 and individual block diagrams show placement for appliqués and embellishments. Finish appliqué edges with machine satin stitch or decorative stitching as desired.

Garden Lily Block

1. Sew 1½" x 12½" First Border strips to top and bottom of 12½" x 23½" Garden Lily Background piece. Press seams toward border. Sew 1½" x 25½" First Border strips to sides. Press.

2. Sew 2½" x 14½" Second Border strips to top and bottom, and 2½" x 29½" Second Border strips to sides of unit. Press seams toward First Border strips.

3. Refer to Quick Fuse Appliqué on page 109. Trace Garden Lily Petal and Garden Lily Leaf Patterns on pages 100-101. Cut required number of each piece from assorted scraps.

4. Referring to Couching Technique on page 111 and block layout, curve green cording for stems and couch in place. Referring to photo on page 92 and layout, position and fuse appliqués on unit. Finish appliqué edges with machine satin stitch or decorative stitching as desired. Garden Lily Block measures 18½" x 29½".

Snail Block

1. Sew 1½" x 16½" Border Fabric strips to top and bottom of 7½" x 16½" Snail Background piece. Press seams toward borders. Sew 1½" x 9½" Border Fabric strips to sides. Press.

2. Refer to Quick Fuse Appliqué on page 109. Trace snail, flower, and grass patterns on page 101. Cut required number of each piece from assorted scraps.

3. Referring to block layout, position and fuse appliqués on unit from step 1. Finish appliqué edges as desired.

4. Refer to Embroidery Stitch Guide on page 111 and pattern on page 101. Use three strands of tan embroidery floss and a stem stitch to embroider snail shell, two strands of tan floss and stem stitch for antennae, two strands of black floss and French knot for eye. Use three strands of green floss and a stem stitch for flower stems. Referring to Couching Technique on page 111 and layout, curve dark green cording under grass appliqués and couch in place. Snail Block measures 18½" x 9½".

Favorite Flowers Lap Quilt
Finished size: 47½" x 58½"
Photo: page 92

Vine Block

1. Refer to Embroidery Stitch Guide on page 111, photo on page 92, and layout. Use three strands of green embroidery floss and a stem stitch to embroider curved vine on 20½" x 4½" Vine Background piece.

2. Refer to Quick Fuse Appliqué on page 109. Trace Vine Leaf Pattern on page 102. Cut five leaves from assorted scraps.

3. Position and fuse appliqués on unit from step 1. Finish appliqué edges as desired.

Geranium Block

1. Sew 1" x 10½" First Border strips to top and bottom of 10½" x 16½" Geranium Background piece. Press seams toward border. Sew 1" x 17½" First Border strips to sides. Press.

2. Sew 2" x 11½" Second Border strips to top and bottom of unit and 2" x 20½" Second Border strips to sides. Press seams toward First Border strips.

3. Refer to Quick Fuse Appliqué on page 109. Trace Large Geranium and Geranium Leaves Patterns on page 100. Mirror-image the Half Flowerpot Pattern to trace complete flowerpot pieces. Cut required number of each piece from assorted scraps.

4. Referring to block layout, position and fuse appliqués on unit from step 2. Finish appliqué edges as desired. Geranium petals will be made and attached to quilt in Layering and Finishing page 99, step 5. Geranium Block measures 14½" x 20½".

creative concepts

Floral Wall Quilts
Various Finished Sizes

Small quilts made from individual blocks from the Favorite Flowers Lap Quilt, pages 94-102, are ideal to add a special touch to any home decor. To add decorator interest to a room, arrange a grouping of two or three individual wall quilts. The Lily Block and Potted Daisies Block complement each other and can fill a larger area on the wall, or add a splash of color by displaying a trio of quilts such as the Geranium Block, Daisy Block, and Viola Block.

Materials Needed

Refer to Floral Sampler Lap Quilt Fabric Chart on page 94 for individual block requirements and the following materials for backing and finishing. Cut binding yardage into 2¾" x 42" strips. Lightweight fusible web will be needed for each block; quantity will be determined by selected block appliqué patterns.

Garden Lily Block
Finished size 19" x 30"
  Binding - ⅓ yard
  Backing - ⅔ yard
  Batting - 23" x 34"
  Green Cording - 1 yard
  Nine Assorted Red beads

Snail Block
Finished size 19" x 10"
  Binding - ¼ yard
  Backing - ½ yard
  Batting - 23" x 14"
  Dark Green Cording ⅜ yard
  Tan, Green, and Black Embroidery Floss
  Three Yellow Beads

Geranium Block
Finished size 15" x 21"
  Binding - ¼ yard
  Backing - ⅝ yard
  Batting - 19" x 25"
  Heavyweight Fusible Web - ⅛ yard
  Twenty-one Black Beads

Potted Daisies Block
Finished size 28" x 19"
  Binding - ⅓ yard
  Backing - ⅔ yard
  Batting - 32" x 23"
  Seven Assorted Black Buttons

Daisy Block
Finished size 10" square
  Binding - ⅛ yard
  Backing - ⅜ yard
  Batting - 13½" square
  Red Cording - 1 yard

Viola Block
Finished size 10" square
  Binding - ⅛ yard
  Backing - ⅜ yard
  Batting - 13½" square

To Make a Small Wall Qu

1. Follow selected block instructions pages 95-98 to construct block.

2. Arrange and baste backing, battir and top together, referring to Layering the Quilt on page 110. Machine or hand quilt as desired. Refer to Binding the Quilt on pag 110 and bind quilt to finish, using 2¾"-wide strips.

Potted Daisies Block

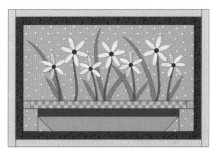

1. Refer to Quick Corner Triangles on page 108. Sew one 2½" Background square to each end of 2½" × 19½" Flowerpot strip as shown. Press.

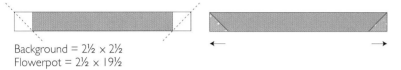

Background = 2½ × 2½
Flowerpot = 2½ × 19½

2. Sew 1½" × 19½" Pot Accent strip to unit from step 1 as shown. Press.

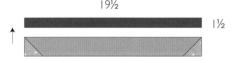

19½

1½

3. Sew unit from step 2 between two 2½" × 3½" Background pieces as shown. Press.

2½   2½

3½

4. Sew 1½" × 21½" Pot Rim strip between two 1½" Background squares as shown. Press.

1½   21½   1½

1½

5. Sew unit from step 4 between 10½" × 23½" Background strip and unit from step 3 as shown. Press.

23½

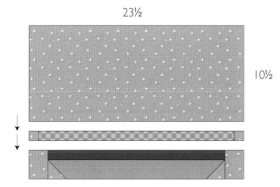

10½

6. Sew 1½" × 23½" First Border strips to top and bottom of unit from step 5. Press seams toward border. Sew 1½" × 16½" First Border strips to sides. Press.

7. Sew 1½" × 25½" Second Border strips to top and bottom of unit from step 6 and 1½" × 18½" Second Border strips to sides. Press seams toward First Border strips.

8. Refer to Quick Fuse Appliqué on page 109. Trace daisy, stem, and leaf patterns on page 102. Cut required number of each piece from assorted scraps. Referring to block layout, position and fuse appliqués on unit. Finish appliqué edges as desired. Potted Daisies Block measures 27½" × 18½".

Daisy Block

1. Refer to Quick Fuse Appliqué on page 109. Trace Daisy and Leaf Patterns on page 105. Cut required number of each piece from assorted scraps.

2. Referring to block layout, position and fuse appliqués on 9½" Daisy Background square. Finish appliqué edges as desired.

3. Referring to Couching Technique on page 111 and layout, arrange red cording to form curve around daisy appliqué, allowing for ¼"-wide seam allowance around block perimeter. Couch cording in place.

creative woman
GARDENS

Viola Block

1. Refer to Quick Corner Triangles on page 108. Sew two 5" Accent Corner squares to opposite corners of 9½" Viola Background square as shown. Press. Sew two 5" Accent Corner squares to remaining corners. Press.

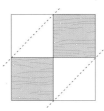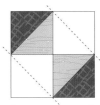

Accent Corners = 5 x 5
Background = 9½ x 9½

2. Refer to Quick Fuse Appliqué on page 109. Trace Viola Patterns. Cut one of each piece from assorted scraps.

3. Position and fuse appliqués on unit from step 1. Finish appliqué edges as desired. Viola Block measures 9½" square.

Viola Pattern

Patterns are reversed for use with Quick-Fuse Appliqué (page 109).

Tracing Line_____
Tracing Line _ _ _ _ _ _ _ _ _ _ _
(will be hidden behind other fabrics)

Whether spending a day with your favorite seed catalog, or taking a well-deserved break from planting, you'll find this posie-covered throw the perfect gardener's companion.

Assembly

1. **Section 1:** Sew Vine Block to Geranium Block. Press. Sew Snail Block to this unit as shown. Press.

2. Sew Garden Lily Block to unit from step 1 as shown. Press.

3. **Section 2:** Sew Daisy Block to Viola Block. Press. Sew Potted Daisies Block to this unit as shown. Press.

4. Referring to photo on page 98 and layout on page 95, sew Section 1 to Section 2. Press.

Borders

1. Sew 2" × 42" Quilt First Border strips end-to-end to make one continuous 2"-wide strip. Press. Refer to Adding the Borders on page 110. Measure quilt through center from side to side. Cut two 2"-wide Quilt First Border strips to that measurement. Sew to top and bottom of quilt. Press seams toward border.

2. Measure quilt through center from top to bottom, including borders just added. Cut two 2"-wide Quilt First Border strips to that measurement. Sew to sides of quilt. Press.

3. Refer to steps 1 and 2 to join, measure, trim, and sew 1¼"-wide Quilt Second Border strips and 3½"-wide Outside Border strips to top, bottom, and sides of quilt. Press seams toward border just added.

Section 1

Section 2

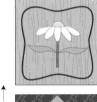

Layering and Finishing

1. Cut backing crosswise into two equal pieces. Sew pieces together to make one 54" × 80" (approximate) backing piece. Press and trim to 54" × 65".

2. Arrange and baste backing, batting, and top together, referring to Layering the Quilt on page 110. Hand or machine quilt as desired.

3. Sew 2¾" × 42" binding strips end-to-end to make one continuous 2¾"-wide strip. Press. Refer to Binding the Quilt on page 110 and bind quilt to finish.

4. Refer to photo on page 92 and layout on page 95. Sew three red beads to each Garden Lily flower, one yellow bead to each Snail Block flower, and assorted black buttons to each daisy in Potted Daisies Block.

5. Refer to Quick Fuse Appliqué on page 109. Using heavyweight fusible web, trace Geranium Petal Pattern on page 100. Fuse and cut twenty-one petal pieces from assorted scraps. Fuse each petal piece to wrong side of matching fabric scrap. Cut out petals. Referring to Geranium Flower Pattern on page 100, attach seven petals to each large flower by sewing a tiny black bead through center of each petal.

creative woman **GARDENS**

Geranium Flower and Leaves Pattern

Patterns are reversed for use with Quick-Fuse Appliqué (page 109).

Tracing Line ———————
Tracing Line - - - - - - - - - - - - - - -
(will be hidden behind other fabrics)
Placement Line — — — — — —
Embroidery Line ....

Large Geranium

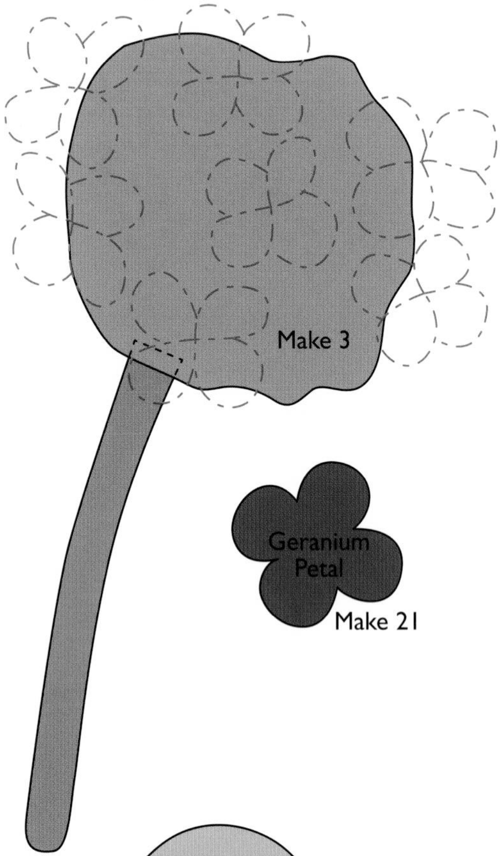

Make 3
Geranium Petal
Make 21

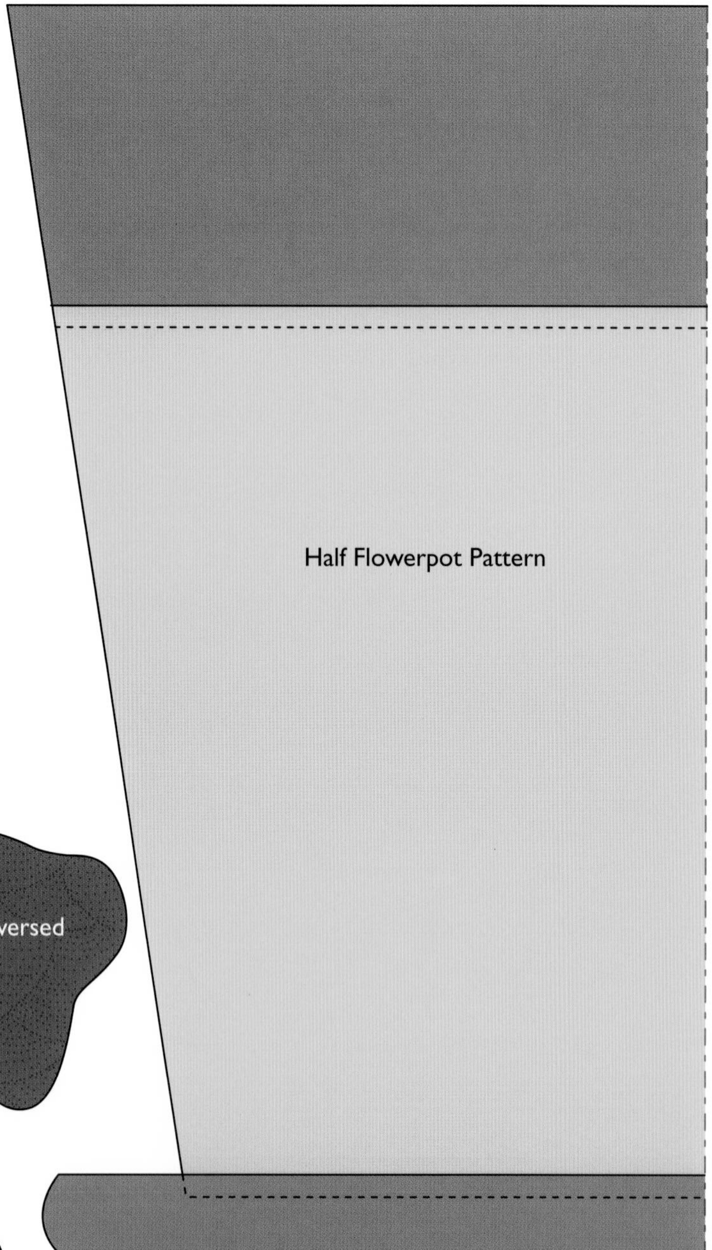

Half Flowerpot Pattern

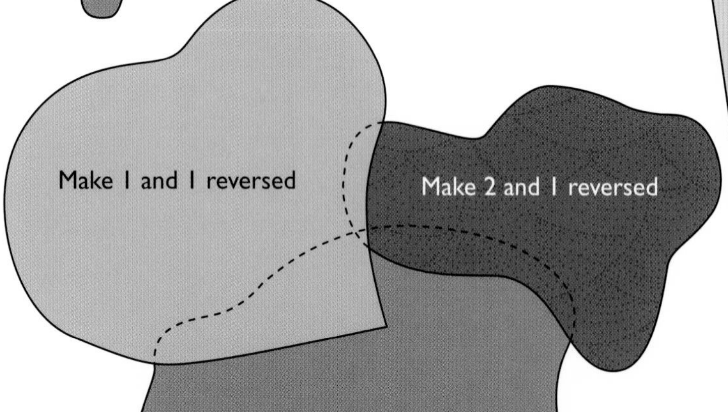

Make 1 and 1 reversed
Make 2 and 1 reversed
Geranium Leaves
Make 2 and 1 reversed

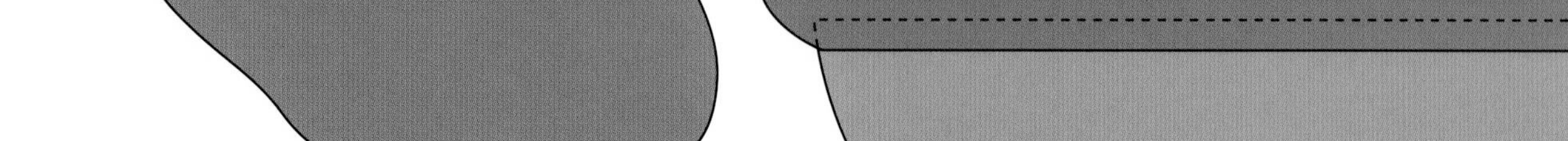

Garden Lily Leaf Pattern
Make 2
and 1 reversed

Garden Lily Pattern
Make 3

Snail Block Pattern

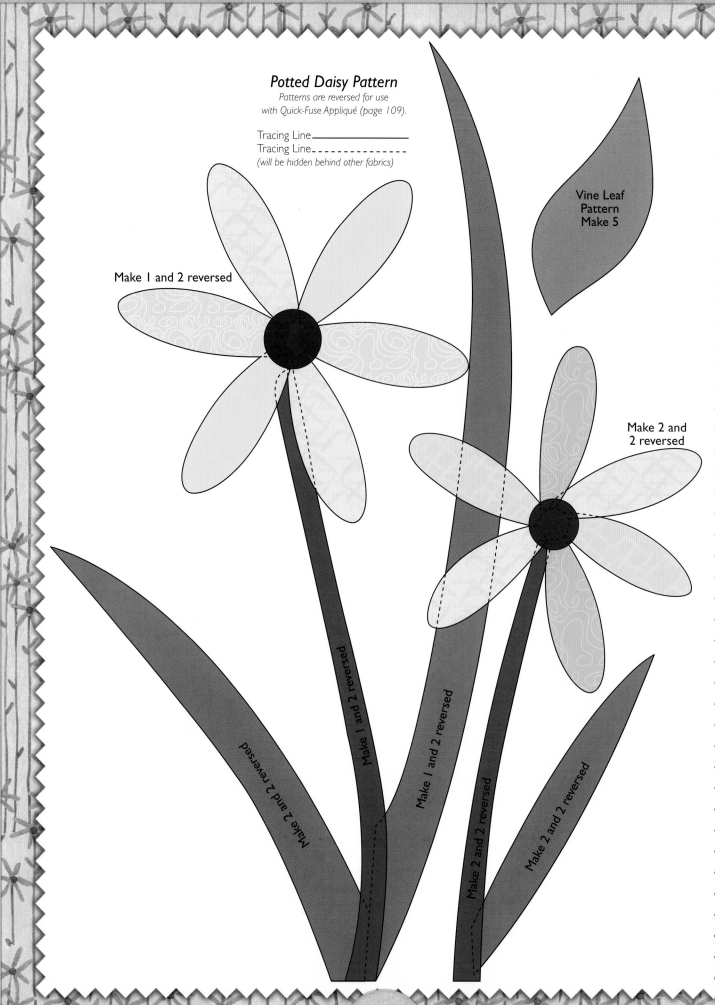

Potted Daisy Pattern

*Patterns are reversed for use
with Quick-Fuse Appliqué (page 109).*

Tracing Line _____
Tracing Line - - - - - - - - - -
(will be hidden behind other fabrics)

Make 1 and 2 reversed

Vine Leaf
Pattern
Make 5

Make 2 and
2 reversed

Make 1 and 2 reversed

Make 1 and 2 reversed

Make 2 and 2 reversed

Make 2 and 2 reversed

Make 2 and 2 reversed

Painted Potting Bench

Prized for its usefulness as both working space and an organizational tool, a potting bench can be as decorative as it is useful. Placed on a porch, patio, or deck, the potting bench can be both pretty and practical.

Materials Needed

Purchased or Handmade Potting Bench

Assorted Paintbrushes

Acrylic Craft Paints - green, light green, blue, light tan

Water-Based Burnt Umber Glaze

Graphite Paper and Pencil

Tracing Paper

Ruler

Finishing Sander and Fine Sandpaper or 150-Grit Sandpaper

Matte Exterior Varnish

Getting Started

Potting benches can be purchased at many home improvement and garden stores or make one yourself. Primitive construction is a decorative plus in a potting bench, so even novice woodworkers can make one as a do-it-yourself project. Plans for potting benches are available at many home improvement stores, or check your local library or the Internet for plans and ideas.

Painting the Potting Bench

1. If the potting bench has been previously painted or stained, sand to remove any sheen and remove sanding residue with damp cloth.

2. Determine placement of each paint color by using the design elements of potting bench as a guide. We chose to paint the back of the upper shelves and the lower shelf with blue paint; the shelf, top, countertop, and fascia board with green paint; and the rest with tan paint. Two coats of paint may be needed for good coverage. Allow paint to dry thoroughly between applications.

3. Trace Vine Leaf Pattern on page 102 onto tracing paper. Referring to photo for placement, transfer leaf designs onto fascia board using graphite paper and pencil. Draw a vine to connect leaves. Using light green paint, paint leaves and vine. Allow to dry.

4. To add checks, paint area tan and allow to dry. Measure length of space to determine width of checks. Use a pencil and ruler to mark off checks. Paint every other square with green paint. Allow to dry.

5. If desired, lightly sand all surfaces with a finishing sander and fine sandpaper to distress the paint. This rustic look is perfect for a roughly constructed potting bench. Remove sanding residue with damp cloth.

6. Apply Burnt Umber Glaze to painted surface following manufacturer's directions.

7. Paint or spray on several coats of matte exterior varnish following manufacturer's directions.

Garden Delights Wall Art

Finished size: 12" x 12"

Garden wall art will add a touch of whimsy to your room and is quick and easy to accomplish. Just paint a stretched canvas and then adhere fabric to add the flower details.

1. Slide interlocking stretcher bars together. Check for square by measuring from corner to corner; repeat for other side, and adjust if necessary. Staple at corners.

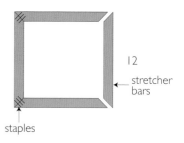

2. Place 18" canvas square under bar unit from step 1. Pull fabric around bar, staple in the middle of each stretcher bar, pulling canvas tightly to obtain good tension. Continue process, working from center, stretching and stapling canvas, stopping at corners.

Back View

Materials Needed
(to make one)

Purchased Stretched Canvas OR Stretcher Bars -
  Four pre-made 12" bars
  One 18" square Canvas

Staple Gun and Staples

2"-wide Bristle Paintbrush

Gesso

Acrylic Paint - Bright green

Background Appliqué -
  One 6" square

Flower and Leaf Appliqués -
  Assorted scraps

Heavyweight Fusible Web -
  ⅛ yard

Appliqué Pressing Sheet (optional)

Fabric Adhesive

Hanger

Preparing the Stretched Canvas

Pre-made stretched canvas comes in a variety of sizes and is available at craft and art supply stores. If you cannot find a canvas in the desired size, purchase stretcher bars that interlock in the correct sizes. We chose 12" lengths to make a 12" square canvas.

3. Pull corner tight and check front to make sure there are no ruffles in canvas. Fold excess fabric at 90°, crease, and form corner. Staple tightly to back.

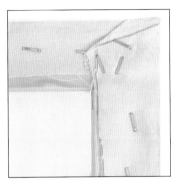

4. Paint Gesso on canvas, covering front and side surfaces as shown. Allow to dry.

Painting the Canvas

1. Mix bright green paint with an equal amount of water. Using a 2"-wide bristle brush, brush the paint on the prepared canvas. Keep strokes loose—coverage should not be solid, but have dark spots and light spots for more interest. Paint front and sides of canvas and allow to dry. If color is too light, repeat the process. If color is too dark, sand lightly with fine sandpaper to take down the color.

Adding the Appliqués

1. Refer to Daisy Pattern below or Potted Daisy Pattern on page 102, quick fuse appliqué on page 109, and photo on page 104. Using heavyweight fusible web, trace and cut daisy and leaf from selected pattern.

2. Referring to Appliqué Pressing Sheet on page 109, arrange and fuse appliqué flower pieces together. Remove from pressing sheet when cool.

3. Fuse web to wrong side of 6" Background Appliqué square, trim piece to 5" square.

4. Using appliqué pressing sheet, arrange and fuse flower and leaf unit from step 4 to Background Appliqué square.

5. Following manufacturer's directions, apply fabric adhesive to back of appliqués and position onto painted canvas. Let adhesive dry thoroughly prior to hanging wall art.

6. Add your choice of hanger to the back of the canvas and hang as desired.

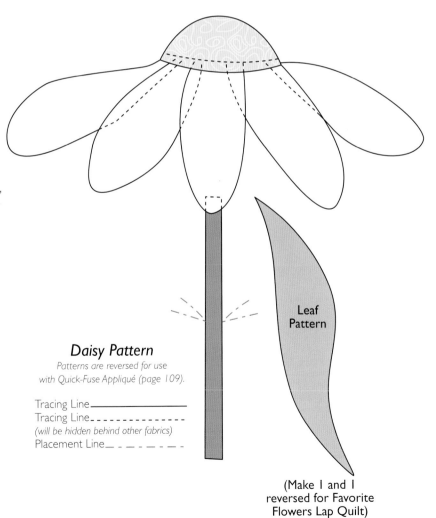

Daisy Pattern

Patterns are reversed for use with Quick-Fuse Appliqué (page 109).

Tracing Line _____
Tracing Line - - - - - - - - - -
(will be hidden behind other fabrics)
Placement Line _ _ _ _ _ _ _

Leaf Pattern

(Make 1 and 1 reversed for Favorite Flowers Lap Quilt)

creative woman
GARDENS

Pop-up Flower Pillow

Finished size: 19" x 19"

You'll love the "touch-me" texture of this delightful pillow—the perfect decorator accent for your bedroom, sofa, or front-porch rocking chair. Make one for yourself and another for a favorite flower-loving friend!

Cutting Instructions

Read all instructions before beginning and use ¼"-wide seam allowances throughout. Read Cutting Strips and Pieces on page 108 prior to cutting fabrics.

Getting Started

A single ruched flower marks the center of this 19" square, single-block pillow, framed with a double-set of narrow borders. Stems are couched with green cording. The leaves are added with fusible appliqué and finished with decorative machine stitching. Press seams in direction of arrows.

Making the Block

1. Refer to Quick-Corner Triangles on page 108. Sew two 7½" Fabric B squares to opposite corners of 14½" Fabric A square as shown. Press. Sew two 7½" Fabric B squares to remaining corners. Press.

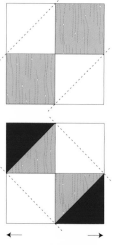

B = 7½ x 7½
A = 14½ x 14½

Pop-up Flower Pillow 19" x 19"	FIRST CUT		SECOND CUT	
	Number of Strips or Pieces	Dimensions	Number of Pieces	Dimensions
Fabric A *Background* ½ yard	1	14½" square		
Fabric B *Accent Triangles* ¼ yard	1	7½" x 42"	4	7½" squares
BORDERS				
Accent Border and Ruched Flower ⅙ yard	1 2	2" x 42" 1" x 42"	2 2	1" x 15½" 1" x 14½"
Outside Border and Backing ⅝ yard	1 2	12½" x 42" 2½" x 42"	2 2 2	12½" x 19½" 2½" x 19½" 2½" x 15½"

Leaf Appliqués - Assorted scraps
Lining/Batting - One 22½" square each
Green Cording - ⅔ yard
Lightweight Fusible Web - Scrap
One ⅝" Button
19" Pillow Form

The Creative Woman By Debbie Mumm®

2. Sew 1" x 14½" Accent Border strips to top and bottom of unit from step 1. Press seams toward border. Sew 1" x 15½" strips to sides. Press.

3. Sew 2½" x 15½" Outside Border strips to top and bottom of unit from step 2. Press seams toward border. Sew 2½" x 19½" strips to sides. Press.

Ruched Flower

1. Place 2" x 42" flower strip right side down and fold long raw edges to meet at center. Press. Fold in half lengthwise and press. Strip should measure ½" wide.

2. With pencil, mark bottom edge of strip at 1" intervals. Mark top edge at 1" intervals starting ½" from end.

double fold

single fold

3. Beginning with the top edge, use ⅛"-long stitches to hand-baste from top mark to bottom mark and back to the next top mark, forming a zigzag pattern. Gently pull thread tightly, gathering fabric to approximately one-third of original length, forming a row of petal-like shapes. Knot end of thread.

4. Coil three petal shapes to form flower center. Stitch to secure in place. Continue coiling gathered strip around center until flower is desired size. Secure and tuck under raw ends.

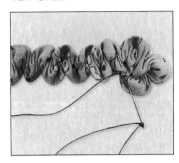

Adding Embellishments

Refer to appliqué instructions on page 109. Our instructions are for quick fuse appliqué. If you prefer hand appliqué, reverse pattern and add ¼"-wide seam allowances.

1. Trace Vine Leaf Pattern on page 102. Cut four leaves from green scraps.

2. Mark center of pillow top. Refer to photo on page 106, layout below, and Couching Technique on page 111, to couch green cording for stems. Appliqué one leaf to end of each stem. Finish edges of leaves with machine satin stitch or decorative stitching as desired.

Layering and Finishing

1. Refer to Finishing Pillows on page 111, step 1, to layer and quilt pillow top.

2. Hand-stitch ruched flower to center of pillow. Sew button to center of flower.

3. Refer to Finishing Pillows on page 111 steps 2-4 to sew backing and make pillow form, if desired.

Pop-up Flower Pillow
Finished size: 19" x 19"
Photo: page 106

creative woman **GARDENS**

General Directions

Cutting Strips and Pieces

We recommend washing cotton fabrics in cold water and pressing before making projects in this book. Using a rotary cutter, see-through ruler, and a cutting mat, cut the strips and pieces for the project. If indicated on the Cutting Chart, some will need to be cut again into smaller strips and pieces. Make second cuts in order shown to maximize use of fabric. The approximate width of the fabric is 42". Measurements for all pieces include ¼"-wide seam allowance unless otherwise indicated. Press in the direction of the arrows.

Fussy Cut

To make a "fussy cut," carefully position ruler or template over a selected design in fabric. Include seam allowances before cutting desired pieces.

Assembly Line Method

Whenever possible, use an assembly line method. Position pieces right sides together and line up next to sewing machine. Stitch first unit together, then continue sewing others without breaking threads. When all units are sewn, clip threads to separate. Press in direction of arrows.

Accurate Seam Allowance

Accurate seam allowances are always important, but especially when the quilt top contains multiple pieced borders with lots of blocks and seams! If each seam is off as little as ⅟₁₆", you'll soon find yourself struggling with components that just won't fit.

To ensure seams are a perfect ¼"-wide, try this simple test: Cut three strips of fabric, each exactly 1½" x 12". With right sides together, and long raw edges aligned, sew two strips together, carefully maintaining a ¼" seam. Press. Add the third strip to complete the strip set. Press seams to one side and measure. The finished strip set should measure 3½" x 12". The center strip should measure 1"-wide, the two outside strips 1¼"-wide, and the seam allowances exactly ¼".

If your measurements differ, check to make sure that seams have been pressed flat. If strip set still doesn't "measure up," try stitching a new strip set, adjusting the seam allowance until a perfect ¼"-wide seam is achieved.

Pressing is very important for accurate seam allowances. Press seams using either steam or dry heat and an "up and down" motion. Do not use side-to-side motion as this will distort the unit or block. Set the seam by pressing along the line of stitching, then press seams to one side as indicated by project instructions.

Quick Corner Triangles

Quick corner triangles are formed by simply sewing fabric squares to other squares or rectangles. The directions and diagrams with each project illustrate what size pieces to use and where to place squares on the corresponding piece. Follow steps 1–3 below to make quick corner triangle units.

1. With pencil and ruler, draw diagonal line on wrong side of fabric square that will form the triangle. See Diagram A. This will be your **sewing** line.

A.

sewing line

2. With right sides together, place square on corresponding piece. Matching raw edges, pin in place, and sew ON drawn line. Trim off excess fabric, leaving ¼"-wide seam allowance as shown in Diagram B.

B.

trim ¼" away
from sewing line

3. Press seam in direction of arrow as shown in step-by-step project diagram. Measure completed corner triangle unit to ensure the greatest accuracy.

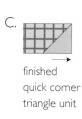

C.

finished
quick corner
triangle unit

Quick-Fuse Appliqué

Quick-fuse appliqué is a method of adhering appliqué pieces to a background with fusible web. For quick and easy results, simply quick-fuse appliqué pieces in place. Use sewable, lightweight fusible web for the projects in this book unless otherwise indicated. Finishing raw edges with stitching is desirable; laundering is not recommended unless edges are finished.

1. With paper side up, lay fusible web over appliqué design. Leaving ½" space between pieces, trace all elements of design. Cut around traced pieces, approximately ¼" outside traced line. See Diagram A.

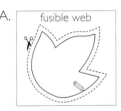
A. fusible web

2. With paper side up, position and press fusible web to wrong side of selected fabrics. Follow manufacturer's directions for iron temperature and fusing time. Cut out each piece on traced line. See Diagram B.

B. fabric-wrong side

3. Remove paper backing from pieces. A thin film will remain on wrong side of fabric. Position and fuse all pieces of one appliqué design at a time onto background, referring to photos for placement. Fused design will be the reverse of traced pattern.

Appliqué Pressing Sheet

An appliqué pressing sheet is very helpful when there are many small elements to apply using a quick-fuse appliqué technique. The pressing sheet allows small items to be bonded together before applying them to the background. The sheet is coated with a special material that prevents the fusible web from adhering permanently to the sheet. Follow manufacturer's directions. Remember to let the fabric cool completely before lifting it from the appliqué sheet. If not cooled, the fusible web could remain on the sheet instead of on the fabric.

Machine Appliqué

This technique should be used when you are planning to launder quick-fuse projects. Several different stitches can be used: small narrow zigzag stitch, satin stitch, blanket stitch, or another decorative machine stitch. Use an open toe appliqué foot if your machine has one. Use a stabilizer to obtain even stitches and help prevent puckering. Always practice first to check machine settings.

1. Fuse all pieces following Quick-Fuse Appliqué directions.

2. Cut a piece of stabilizer large enough to extend beyond the area to be stitched. Pin to the wrong side of fabric.

3. Select thread to match appliqué.

4. Following the order that appliqués were positioned, stitch along the edges of each section. Anchor beginning and ending stitches by tying off or stitching in place two or three times.

5. Complete all stitching, then remove stabilizer.

Hand Appliqué

Hand appliqué is easy when you start out with the right supplies. Cotton or machine embroidery thread is easy to work with. Pick a color that matches the appliqué fabric as closely as possible. Use appliqué or silk pins for holding shapes in place and a long, thin needle, such as a sharp, for stitching.

1. Make a template for every shape in the appliqué design. Use a dotted line to show where pieces overlap.

2. Place template on right side of appliqué fabric. Trace around template.

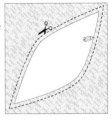

3. Cut out shapes ¼" beyond traced line.

4. Position shapes on background fabric, referring to quilt layout. Pin shapes in place.

5. When layering and stitching appliqué shapes, always work from background to foreground. Where shapes overlap, do not turn under and stitch edges of bottom pieces. Turn and stitch the edges of the piece on top.

6. Use the traced line as your turn-under guide. Entering from the wrong side of the appliqué shape, bring the needle up on the traced line. Using the tip of the needle, turn under the fabric along the traced line. Using blind stitch, stitch along the folded edge to join the appliqué shape to the background fabric. Turn under and stitch about ¼" at a time.

Making Bias Strips

1. Refer to Fabric Requirements and Cutting Instructions for the amount of fabric required for the specific bias needed.

2. Remove selvages from the fabric piece and cut into a square. Mark edge with straight pin where selvages were removed as shown. Cut square once diagonally into two equal 45° triangles. (For larger squares, fold square in half diagonally and gently press fold. Open fabric square and cut on fold.)

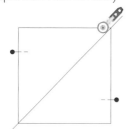

3. Place pinned edges right sides together and stitch along edge with a ¼" seam. Press seam open.

4. Using a ruler and rotary cutter, cut bias strips to width specified in quilt directions.

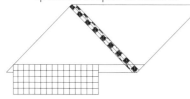

5. Each strip has a diagonal end. To join, place strips perpendicular to each other, right sides together, matching diagonal cut edges and allowing tips of angles to extend approximately ¼" beyond edges. Sew ¼"-wide seams. Continue stitching ends together to make the desired length. Press seams open. Cut strips into recommended lengths according to quilt directions.

Adding the Borders

1. Measure quilt through the center from side to side. Trim two border strips to this measurement. Sew to top and bottom of quilt. Press seams toward border.

2. Measure quilt through the center from top to bottom, including borders added in step 1. Trim border strips to this measurement. Sew to sides and press. Repeat to add additional borders.

Layering the Quilt

1. Cut backing and batting 4" to 8" larger than quilt top.

2. Lay pressed backing on bottom (right side down), batting in middle, and pressed quilt top (right side up) on top. Make sure everything is centered and that backing and batting are flat. Backing and batting will extend beyond quilt top.

3. Begin basting in center and work toward outside edges. Baste vertically and horizontally, forming a 3"– 4" grid. Baste or pin completely around edge of quilt top. Quilt as desired. Remove basting.

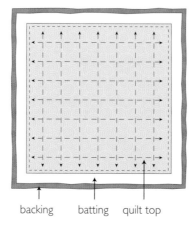

backing   batting   quilt top

Binding the Quilt

1. Trim batting and backing to ¼" beyond raw edge of quilt top. This will add fullness to binding.

2. Fold and press binding strips in half lengthwise with wrong sides together.

3. Measure quilt through center from side to side. Cut two binding strips to this measurement. Lay binding strips on top and bottom edges of quilt top with raw edges of binding and quilt top aligned. Sew through all layers, ¼" from quilt edge. Press binding away from quilt top.

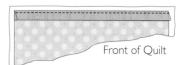

Front of Quilt

4. Measure quilt through center from top to bottom, including binding just added. Cut two binding strips to this measurement and sew to sides through all layers, including binding just added. Press.

5. Folding top and bottom first, fold binding around to back then repeat with sides. Press and pin in position. Hand-stitch binding in place using a blind stitch.

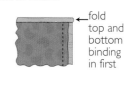

← fold top and bottom binding in first

Finishing Pillows

1. Layer batting between pillow top and lining. Baste. Hand or machine quilt as desired, unless otherwise indicated. Trim batting and lining even with raw edge of pillow top.

2. Narrow hem one long edge of each backing piece by folding under ¼" to wrong side. Press. Fold under ¼" again to wrong side. Press. Stitch along folded edge.

3. With right sides up, lay one backing piece over second piece so hemmed edges overlap, making backing unit the same measurement as the pillow top. Baste backing pieces together at top and bottom where they overlap.

4. With right sides together, position and pin pillow top to backing. Using ¼"-wide seam, sew around edges, trim corners, turn right side out, and press.

Pillow Forms

Cut two pieces of fabric to finished size of pillow form plus ½". Place right sides together, aligning raw edges. Using ¼"-wide seam, sew around all edges, leaving 4" opening for turning. Trim corners and turn right side out. Stuff to desired fullness with polyester fiberfill and hand-stitch opening closed.

Couching Technique

Couching is a method of attaching a textured yarn, cord, or fiber to fabric for decorative purposes. Use an open-toe embroidery foot or a zigzag presser foot and matching or monofilament thread. Sew with a long zigzag stitch just barely wider than the cord or yarn. Stabilizer on the wrong side of fabric is recommended. Place the yarn, cord, or fiber on right side of fabric and zigzag to attach as shown. A hand-stitch can be used if desired.

Couching

Embroidery Stitch Guide

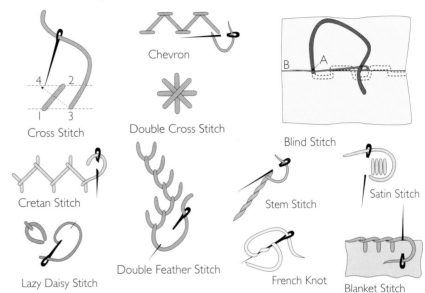

Cross Stitch

Chevron

Double Cross Stitch

Blind Stitch

Cretan Stitch

Double Feather Stitch

Stem Stitch

Satin Stitch

Lazy Daisy Stitch

French Knot

Blanket Stitch

Special Thanks~

We wish to extend special thanks to the creative women who are quoted and/or pictured in our chapter introductions:

Quilts ~ *Julie Lee Gutierrez as a baby with her inspirational grandmother Viola Agnes Schenk and sisters Teresa Lee Grundman and Laura Lee Linder (1968); Detail of crazy quilt owned by Carolyn Ogden.*

Scrapbooks ~ *Crop Night photo: Mya Brooks, Georgie Gerl, Heather Butler, Sabrina Gonder, Kris Clifford, and Kathy Eisenbarth; Baby quilt photo: Kathy Rickel with Baby Brian's quilt.*

Cooks ~*The Soup Kitchen: Jackie Saling, Maggie Bullock, Cyndi Tobias, Lou McKee, Pam Mostek, Jean Van Bockel; Soup Kitchen Quilt.*

Relaxes ~ *Quilter Margie Karavitas; Detail of Margie's handwork.*

Stitches ~ *Monique Scritchfield and Marga House; Heather and Joe Butler with embroidered baby quilt.*

Enjoys Nature ~ *Karen Schoepflin Hagen with one of her quilts; Forest Floor Fragment by Karen Schoepflin Hagen.*

Decorates ~ *Debbie Mumm in the process of redecorating her living room.*

Gardens ~ *Quilter and Master Gardener Sue Bates; Maureen Cramer, quilter and gardener.*

Discover More from Debbie Mumm®

Here's a sampling of the many quilting and home décor books by Debbie Mumm®. These books are available at your local quilt shop, by calling (888) 819-2923, or by shopping online at www.debbiemumm.com.

Debbie Mumm's®
Best Loved Quilting Themes
112-page, soft cover

Debbie Mumm's®
Decorating with Quick & Easy Quilts
112-page, soft cover

new!

Debbie's latest books feature enclosed wire binding so instructions and patterns lay flat!

Debbie Mumm's®
Quilts from a Gardener's Journal
112-page, soft cover

Debbie Mumm's® Decorating with Quick & Easy Holiday Quilts
112-page, soft cover

Debbie Mumm's®
Cozy Northwest Christmas
112-page, soft cover

Debbie Mumm, Inc.
1116 E. Westview Court
Spokane, WA 99218

DEBBIE MUMM

Toll Free (888) 819-2923
(509) 466-3572
Fax (509) 466-6919

www.debbiemumm.com

Credits

Designs by Debbie Mumm®

Special thanks to my creative teams:

Editorial and Project Design

Carolyn Ogden: Managing Editor
Georgie Gerl: Quilt and Craft Designer
Carolyn Lowe: Quilt and Craft Designer
Nancy Kirkland: Seamstress/Quilter
Darra Williamson: Writer
Laura M. Reinstatler: Technical Editor
Maggie Bullock: Copy Editor
Jackie Saling: Craft Designer
Kris Clifford: Craft Designer
Pam Clarke: Machine Quilter
Wanda Jeffries: Machine Quilter

Book Design and Production

Mya Brooks: Production Director
Tom Harlow: Graphics Manager
Heather Hughes: Graphic Designer
Robert H. Fitzner: Graphic Designer
Kathy Rickel: Art Studio Assistant

Photography

Peter Hassel Photography
Debbie Mumm® Graphics Studio

Art Team

Lou McKee: Senior Artist/Designer
Kathy Arbuckle: Artist/Designer
Sandy Ayars: Artist
Heather Butler: Artist
Gil-Jin Foster: Artist
Kathy Eisenbarth: Artist

The Debbie Mumm® Sewing Studio exclusively uses Bernina® sewing machines.

©2004 Debbie Mumm
Printed in Hong Kong